CAPRICORN 2002

Teri King's Astrological
Horoscopes for 2002

♑

Capricorn

**Teri King's complete horoscope
for all those whose birthdays fall
between 22 December and 19 January**

Teri King

Thorsons

Thorsons
An Imprint of HarperCollins*Publishers*
77–85 Fulham Palace Road
Hammersmith, London W6 8JB

The Thorsons website address is: www.thorsons.com

Published by Thorsons 2001

1 3 5 7 9 10 8 6 4 2

A catalogue record for this book
is available from the British Library

ISBN 0 00 712141 5

Printed and bound in Great Britain by
Omnia Books Limited, Glasgow

♑

Contents

Capricorn
22 December to 19 January

Ruling Planet: **Saturn**
Element: **Earth**
Qualities: **Feminine, Negative**
Planetary Principle: **Crystallization**
Primal Desire: **Attainment**
Colours: **Charcoal grey, Black, Green**
Jewel: **Emerald**
Day: **Wednesday**
Magical Number: **Four**

Famous Capricorns
Helena Rubenstein, Richard Nixon, Howard Hughes,
Martin Luther King Jr, Edgar Allan Poe, J Edgar Hoover,
Muhammad Ali, Benjamin Franklin, Humphrey Bogart,
Joan of Arc, Isaac Newton, Marlene Dietrich,
Al Capone, Janis Joplin

℔

Introduction

Astrology has many uses, not least of these its ability to help us to understand both ourselves and other people. Unfortunately there are many misconceptions and confusions associated with it, such as that old chestnut – how can a zodiac forecast be accurate for all the millions of people born under one particular sign?

The answer to this is that all horoscopes published in newspapers, books and magazines are, of necessity, of a general nature. Unless an astrologer can work from the date, time and place of your birth, the reading given will only be true for the typical member of your sign.

For instance, let's take a person born on 9 August. This person is principally a subject of Leo, simply because the Sun occupied that section of the heavens known as Leo during 23 July to 22 August. However, when delving into astrology at its most serious, there are other influences which need to be taken into consideration – for example, the Moon. This planet enters a fresh sign every 48 hours. On the birth date in question it may have been in, say, Virgo. And if this were the case it would make our particular subject Leo (Sun representing willpower) and Virgo (Moon representing instincts) or, if you

℔

will, a Leo/Virgo. Then again the rising sign of 'ascendant' must also be taken into consideration. This also changes constantly as the Earth revolves: approximately every two hours a new section of the heavens comes into view – a new sign passes over the horizon. The rising sign is of the utmost importance, determining the image projected by the subject to the outside world – in effect, the personality.

The time of birth is essential when compiling a birth chart. Let us suppose that in this particular instance Leo was rising at the time of birth. Now, because two of the three main influences are Leo, our sample case would be fairly typical of his or her sign, possessing all the faults and attributes associated with it. However, if the Moon and ascendant had been in Virgo then, whilst our subject would certainly display some of the Leo attributes or faults, it is more than likely that for the most part he or she would feel and behave more like a Virgoan.

As if life weren't complicated enough, this procedure must be carried through to take into account all the remaining planets. The position and signs of Mercury, Venus, Mars, Jupiter, Saturn, Uranus, Neptune and Pluto must all be discovered, plus the aspect formed from one planet to another. The calculation and interpretation of these movements by an astrologer will then produce an individual birth chart.

Because the heavens are constantly changing, people with identical charts are a very rare occurrence. Although it is not inconceivable that it could happen, this would mean that the two subjects were born not only on the same date and at the same time, but also in the same place. Should such an incident occur, then the deciding factors as to how these individuals would differ in their approach to life, love, career, financial prospects and so on, would be due to environmental and parental influence.

℞

Returning to our hypothetical Leo: our example with the rising Sun in Leo and Moon in Virgo may find it useful not only to read up on his or her Sun sign (Leo) but also to read the section dealing with Virgo (the Moon). Nevertheless, this does not invalidate Sun sign astrology. This is because of the great power the Sun possesses, and on any chart this planet plays an important role.

Belief in astrology does not necessarily mean believing in totally determined lives – that our actions are predestined and we have no control over our fate. What it does clearly show is that our lives run in cycles, for both good and bad and, with the aid of astrology, we can make the most of, or minimize, certain patterns and tendencies. How this is done is entirely up to the individual. For example, if you are in possession of the knowledge that you are about to experience a lucky few days or weeks, then you can make the most of them by pushing ahead with plans. You can also be better prepared for illness, misfortune, romantic upset and every adversity.

Astrology should be used as it was originally intended – as a guide, especially to character. In this direction it is invaluable and it can help us in all aspects of friendship, work and romance. It makes it easier for us to see ourselves as we really are and, what's more, as others see us. We can recognize both our own weaknesses and strengths and those of others. It can give us both outer confidence and inner peace.

In the following pages you will find personality profiles, an in-depth look at the year ahead from all possible angles including numerology, monthly and daily guides, your Sun sign partner, plus, and it is a big plus, information for those poor and confused creatures so often ignored who are born on 'the cusp' – at the beginning or the end of each sign.

Used wisely, astrology can help you through life. It is not intended to encourage complacency, since, in the final analysis, what you do with your life is up to you. This book will aid you in adopting the correct attitude to the year ahead and thus maximize your chances of success. Positive thinking is encouraged because this helps us to attract positive situations. Allow astrology to walk hand in hand with you and you will be increasing your chances of success and happiness.

How Does
Astrology Work?

You often hear people say that there is no scientific explanation for astrology. However, astrological calculations may be explained in a very precise way, and they can be done by anyone with a little practice and a knowledge of the movement of stars and planets. It is the interpretations and conclusions drawn from these observations that are not necessarily consistent or verifiable, and, to be sure, predicted events do not always happen. Yet astrology has lasted in our culture for over 3,000 years, so there must be something in it!

So how can we explain astrology? Well, each individual birth sign has its own set of deep-seated characteristics, and an understanding of these can give you fresh insights into why you behave as you do. Reading an astrological interpretation, even if it is just to find out how, say, a new relationship might develop, means that you should think about yourself in a very deep way. But it is important to remember that the stars don't determine your fate. It is up to you to use them to the best advantage in any situation.

Although astrology, like many other 'alternative' practices such as homeopathy, dowsing and telepathy, cannot completely be explained, there have been convincing experiments that have shown that it works far more often than chance would allow. The best-known studies are those of the French statistician, Michel Gauquelin, whose results were checked by a professor at the University of London who declared, grudgingly, that 'there was something in it'.

An important aspect of astrology is to look at how the Sun and the Moon affect the natural world around us from day to day. For instance, the rise and fall of the tides is purely a result of the movement and position of the Moon relative to the Earth. If this massive magnetic pull can move the oceans of the Earth, what does it do to us? After all, we are, on average, over 60 per cent water!

When it comes to the ways in which the Sun may change the world, a whole book could be written on the subject. The influences we know about include day length, heat, light, solar storms, as well as magnetic, ultra-violet and many other forms of radiation. And all this from over 90 million miles away! For example, observation of birds has shown that before migration – governed by changes in the length of days – birds put on extra layers of fat, and that they experience a nocturnal restlessness shortly before setting off on their travels. I'm not suggesting that we put on weight and experience sleepless nights because of the time of year, but many people will tell you that different seasons affect them in different ways.

Another example from the natural world is a curious species of giant worm which lives in underground caverns in the South Pacific. Twice a year, as the Sun is rising and the tide is at its highest, these worms come to the surface of the ocean. The inhabitants of the islands consider them a great delicacy! There are so many instances of creatures on this planet responding to the influences of the Moon and the Sun that it is only common sense to wonder whether the position of other planets also has an affect, even if it is more subtle and less easy to identify.

Finally, we come to the question of how astrology might work in predicting future events. As we have seen, the planetary bodies are likely to affect us in all sorts of ways, both physically and mentally. Most often, subtle changes in the positions of the planets will cause slight changes in our emotional states and, of course, this will affect how we behave. By drawing up a chart based on precise birth times, and by using their intuition, some astrologers can make precise predictions about how planetary influences in the years ahead are likely to shape the life of an individual. Many people are very surprised at how well an astrologer seems to 'understand' them after reading a commentary on their birth chart!

Stranger still are the astrologers who appear to be able to predict future events many years before they happen. The most famous example of all is the 16th-century French astrologer, Nostradamus, who is well-known for having predicted the possibility of world destruction at the end of the last millennium. Don't worry, I think I can cheerfully put everyone's mind at rest by assuring you that the world will go on for a good many years yet. Although Nostradamus certainly made some very accurate predictions in his lifetime, his prophecies for our future are very obscure and are hotly disputed by all the experts. Mind you, it is quite clear that there are likely to be massive changes ahead. It is a possibility, for instance, that information may come to light about past civilizations, now at the bottom of the Mediterranean Sea: this will give us a good idea about how people once lived in the past, and pointers as to how we should live in the future. Try not to fear, dear reader. Astrology is a tool for us to use and if we use it wisely, no doubt we will survive with greater wisdom and a greater respect for our world and each other.

The Sun in Capricorn

Your motto is that you can never be too rich or too thin. On a strict diet you're the kind of person who would cheat by eating less. That's because you have the discipline of an individual who doesn't know how to dally.

At times you seem frigid and glacial, but that's only to fool people. Your feelings are very much at the forefront. However, so is your sense of duty, and with this nothing dares interfere. There are moments when, in getting done what you have to do, you may appear cold, impatient and condescending. The fact is that you simply have no time for frivolity, aimless chatter or the kind of interference that might disrupt your day.

Your pace is go, go, go, push, push, push, through sickness, depression, physical illness and non-specific disruptions of any nature. In short, you are the most hopeless kind of workaholic who thinks of a holiday as a different kind of work.

Because of your goal-oriented behaviour, you usually get wherever you want to go. And that's to the top, naturally, since you have no tolerance for being second best. However, despite your extraordinary success, you're so self-critical that you can barely believe it once you get there.

On the outside you smile and bow with a devastating dignity as you stoop to scoop up another success symbol. However, on the inside you feel that you are simply fooling your public and that it is just a matter of time until the truth comes oozing out. In an anxiety attack you weigh your attributes against your fatal flaws, which you duly inflate and then agonize about.

You have such a wilted sense of self-worth that it's almost a daily ordeal for you to try to deal with it. That's probably why you work so much, since you need something to take up your attention, or else self-criticism will consume your ego.

You are kind, faithful, responsible and possess the sort of integrity that makes people want to stay in your life. You're usually a long-lasting friend who takes over in painful and needy moments. You can be depended on for your loyalty, sincerity and constant support.

You need a strong person with, preferably, a sense of humour, who is free with their feelings rather than confined by the fear of them. Popular astrology teases the Capricorn for being a status-seeker who would rather marry for money than love – not true. What you really want is a partner who is adept at making you feel real. The immature people who pass through your life never have much luck in the long run; you're too solemn and dignified for their superficiality. You'd rather have a person whose character you can respect and who can laugh at their faults with you. And when you find that love of your life, you will be thrilled that once again your dream has been realized.

The Year Ahead:
Overview

This year Pluto will be sizzling along in the fiery sign of Sagittarius, stimulating many aspects of your character, including faith in human nature, impulsiveness, enthusiasm, wisdom, a sense of perspective, exploration, versatility and joviality. However, there could be occasions when you may become obsessed with independence and freedom. Furthermore, there'll be a compelling need for you to achieve self-discipline. Pluto's placing on your birth chart suggests that you have a vital need to achieve an understanding of life, but you must avoid suppressing your emotions, and learn to control sudden outbursts. There will be a good deal going on behind the scenes, and it's up to you to make sure that you are 'in the know'.

Neptune will be making its way through the airy sign of Aquarius this year. As a result you'll be more responsive to social, political and philosophical stimuli, and your ideals will be humanitarian. Your power to theorize is also strong, but this placing can inflate your love of independence, so that on occasions it could get out of control. This planet will bring gains or losses through hunches, dreams, speculations, the luxury trades and business associated with films, aviation, shipping, alcohol and charities.

Money matters are going to be a bit complicated, and this may bring anxieties on occasion, as you to tend to be rather materialistic. Despite this, there will be times when you are indifferent to money, and you may be careless with it. You're normally very canny about such matters, but from time to time this year you will display little financial acumen and could get yourself into a bit of a mess. Take care that you are not imposed upon by other people who may believe that you are 'an easy mark'.

Uranus, too, will be situated in the air sign of Aquarius. This will help to stimulate originality, understanding and progressive thinking. However, this planet may destroy senti-mentality, and your willpower could be wayward from time to time. Others may try to put you right, but your self-will is strong, even perverse, so it's unlikely that you're going to be listening. Furthermore, there may be gains or losses through unusual sources, such as antiques, windfalls and erratic behaviour. You will be drawn to sudden speculations and gambling. Generally speaking, though, you will acquire a cer-tain amount of independence through your resources, and luckily you'll be able to extricate yourself from emergencies in a thoroughly admirable and ingenious way.

Saturn will be in Gemini all year, and because of this you'll be trying to develop more seriously ordered thinking. You'll realize that you must be more adaptable and versatile. Your reasoning faculties will be strong for this entire period, but try your best to avoid slow thinking, because this will make you irritated with yourself.

Jupiter will be in Cancer up until 1 August, increasing your liking for domesticity as well as your physical appetites for food and sex. Your business acumen is good, and you'll be making some very wise decisions. You'll be able to make your

way around rivals and opponents, whose power to hurt will
turn out to be very ineffective. Remember that your mind is
going to be practical, yet imaginative, but it could sometimes
be just a touch fanciful. Jupiter in Cancer will make you more
sociable and good natured, but it could also encourage you to
be a bit over-generous from time to time, though any partnerships are likely to be beneficial. If you are married, there is a
chance that you may be expanding your family with a new
baby. During this time it seems there's a great deal to look
forward to. All you have to do is recognize the fact and leap
into action at the appropriate time – that's where this little
book comes in.

Jupiter will be moving into Leo on 2 August, where it will
stay for the remainder of the year. That's the area of your chart
devoted to big business, insurance matters and, to a degree,
team effort, so you needn't struggle on alone unless you really
want to. Other people are going to be 'there' for you, so make
life easy on yourself and keep in touch with them.

Career Year

When it comes to work, you rate security above everything else. A regular pay packet is of the utmost importance, because it gives you peace of mind. This should always be remembered when choosing a job. Any scheme to 'get rich quick' would not normally appeal to you, and it will need to be discouraged if it does. You're the kind of person who needs to make progress in a steady way on a long-term basis; when you do this, the sky is the limit, and by hook or by crook you'll reach the top of your profession.

You enjoy success, fame and publicity and your career can be so important to you that sometimes all else is excluded. At some point during life, you're more than likely to be attracted to the ruthless field of politics, but speedy disillusion could make this a brief experience.

Any position or job where your qualities of economy and calm can be exercised and developed will be suitable. A position where you can establish authority, constructive systems of production and administration for the benefit of a community, or business, is just your cup of tea.

You could do well in a wide range of positions, such as scientist, head teacher, manager, civil servant, mathematician, farmer, politician, builder, osteopath, surveyor, architect, dentist or musician.

Despite any drawbacks that you feel you have in your background, you will succeed in life once your mind has been made up – through hard work and sheer determination. Capricorns can often be difficult once they have arrived; they are strongly attracted to big, ambitious projects. You'll feel fully obligated to any contract and will usually fulfil your responsibilities against all odds.

But how will you fare during this particular year? Well, for that we need to refer to the planet of Venus, which rules the professional part of your life.

During January Venus is situated in your own sign, meaning it would be a good idea to mix business with pleasure whenever you possibly can, especially if you are hoping to further your ambitions.

This placing exists up until 18 January, after which Venus will be moving into Aquarius, where it stays until 12 February. During this time, those of you in financial occupations will do exceptionally well, but it would be a good idea to use a softer approach. Take somebody out for a quick drink, even a meal if you can afford it; your solicitous behaviour will get you what you want in the long run.

From 12 February to 7 March, Venus will be coasting along in Pisces. This will certainly be an ideal time for artistic jobs and sales, because you have the gift of the gab and others can be easily persuaded round to your way of thinking. Your mind is bright and inventive and will be making a big impression.

From 8 to 31 March, Venus will be in Aries, in the area of your chart devoted to family matters and jobs which cater to property and items for the home. If your profession takes in any of these, you'll be doing very well indeed.

From 1 to 25 April, Venus is found in Taurus, which brings gains from matters related to higher education and foreign affairs, as well as people from strange lands, so if you hear any foreign accents see if you can get their owners to help you out.

From 26 April to 20 May, Venus is in the airy sign of Gemini. This will be a good time for those who work in the health or beauty industries. You may be rushed off your feet, but you'll find your work more than usually satisfying – surely no bad thing.

From 21 May to 14 June, Venus is in Cancer, and that, of course, is your opposite number. You can expect other people, regardless of their profession, and indeed yours, to be extremely helpful and useful. If you mix business with pleasure as much as you possibly can, you'll be doing yourself a big favour.

From 15 June to 10 July, Venus is found in Leo. There's a rosy glow about insurance matters, banking and the like. If you've got an overdraft, this is the ideal time to sweet-talk your bank manager.

From 11 July to 5 August, Venus can be found in Virgo, a fine earth sign like yourself. This will be a particularly useful time for dealing with foreigners, or doing any business travelling. You'll make a big impression.

From 6 August to 7 September, Venus is located in Libra, the zenith point of your chart. It really doesn't matter what you do for a living, it would be a good idea to mix business with pleasure whenever you possibly can. If your job is at all creative, you're in for a good time.

From 8 September through to the end of the year, Venus makes a slow trip through Scorpio. That's the area of your chart devoted to team effort, friendships and contacts. Don't struggle on alone; other people will be interested (and possibly fascinated) in what you are doing, so confide in them.

℔

♌

Money Year

When it comes to cash, you're usually sensible and can easily become miserly. You can also be trusted to make sound, conservative investments and to account for every penny. However, there are very few born under this sign who make brilliant speculators, because you're too concerned with saving cash to think of a high-risk, high-profit coup. You are, of course, as practical about cash as you are about everything else. You like to see solid results for your labour, and money is a very satisfactory foundation for the kind of result you are looking for. To be fair, you're not much interested in cash for its own sake, but you most certainly want to get somewhere in this world, and you recognize that money will help you do just that. You must admit that you can be careful to the point of meanness on the way up the ladder, but you won't think twice about spending when it comes to furthering your ambitions.

You thoroughly enjoy the idea of mixing business with pleasure, and you generally make a generous host, especially if you're in a position to spend other people's money rather than your own.

Secretly, you admire people born under more dashing signs, who are prepared to put money at risk. You could be

♌

more like them, but you can't bring yourself to risk losing that which you've worked so hard to accumulate, and who can blame you? Mind you, there's a soft and sentimental side to your character: the only time you weaken and are prepared to loosen the purse strings is on special occasions, because you feel you have a valid reason for dipping into your savings. This is probably one of the reasons why you enjoy birthdays, anniversaries and Christmas so much.

But what about your chances of making it really big this year? Well, the planet which needs to be consulted in a general way is Uranus.

Uranus will remain in the sign of Aquarius all year, giving the planet extra power. Although you are always a materialistic person, it's quite likely that this side of your nature could get completely out of control from time to time. The last thing you should do is appear to be money-grabbing, because that will be unattractive to just the people who were prepared to put opportunities your way.

Lastly, do take note when Uranus goes into retrograde movement, because that is when things could get really complicated. You will find this information in the Monthly and Daily Guides.

♑

Love and Sex Year

A Capricorn doesn't fall in love easily, but when you do, you set about determinedly getting the one you want. You're not impulsive, and there's often a sound practical basis for your choice. You don't shirk from the basics of sex; you keep your head and you are not likely to throw yourself away on just anyone, but there's nothing half-hearted in your approach.

You may develop an interest in a possible partner somewhat later in life than the average person, but once you do you form strong, lasting attachments. Your interest in sex is often submerged completely when other interests take up your time. However, when it comes to physical pleasures, you can be lusty and earthy, yet at the same time a little bit cool.

You may spend a considerable amount of your time in the quest for enjoyment and satisfaction. However, you can be very small-minded about it, expecting the other person concerned to follow your desires to the letter. You must try hard not to be selfish, nor to expect more from other people than they can give. You can be jealous and touchy, particularly about people's attitudes towards you. The reason for this is often that you are afraid of being refused, which makes you inclined to be suspicious and to expect the other person to make the first move. Once you are sure of being wanted, however, you feel confident enough to commit yourself completely, but you're still going to need every encouragement before you can relax and really fall in love.

There's no doubt about it, you want to possess your loved one completely and to have them respond by being even more enthusiastic than you are. As long as your intimacy lasts, you are perfectly content to act decently. However, you are very proud, and you can quickly become cool and aloof if you feel rejected. Once you are happily settled, though, you are domestic and faithful and prefer staying at home to a lot of socializing.

Your artistic instincts are not usually very well developed, although this can be modified by the placings on your chart. As a rule, moral beauty appeals to you more than the physical kind.

But what of your chances during the year 2002? Well, Venus is the planet of love, and during January it is in your own sign until the 18th. You look good, feel good and are at your most loving and approachable – so there's a distinct possibility you could meet someone very special at this time. Of course, if you already have a mate you may be tempted to stray, but luckily you have an iron will so should be able to keep this under control. Hopefully you're going to do just that.

From 19 January through to 11 February, Venus will be drifting along in Aquarius, the area of your chart devoted to money and possessions. You may make the mistake of believing that if you spend a lot of cash on someone, they will admire you for it. I'm afraid you could be sorely disappointed. Don't fall for this pitfall.

From 12 February to 7 March, Venus is found in the water sign of Pisces, the area of your chart devoted to short-distance travel and the mind. It'll be relatively easy for you to sweet-talk your way round literally anybody. Furthermore, you'll be prepared to take short trips to visit people you've got a passion for.

From 8 to 31 March, Venus will be in Aries, the area of your chart devoted to home and family. It's unlikely you'll be prepared to travel very far, however you will delight in enter-taining new friends and contacts at home – though, of course, it's not going to lead to romance.

From 1 to 25 April, Venus will be in your own sign, so you're looking good, feeling good and are ready, willing and able to form all kinds of relationships, professional and per-sonal. If you have someone special in your life, this could be the time when you'll be thinking of making that all-important commitment. Engagements and marriages are certainly well-starred, so push ahead.

From 26 April to 20 May, Venus will be in Gemini. Although this may help you on the work front (because your charm will get you everywhere), it's unlikely that serious romance will be taking place. You may start little relationships with work colleagues, only to realize they're not really your cup of tea.

From 21 May to 14 June, Venus will be in Cancer, your opposite number. You can push ahead with romance without fearing that you will fail. All kinds of relationships can be formed at this time, such as engagements, marriages, or perhaps even a business liaison. All in all, you've a lot to look forward to at this time.

From 15 June to 10 July, Venus will be in Leo. You may be attracted to people by their status, which isn't a good thing and so it's not surprising to find that relationships made in this way will not work for very long.

From 11 July to 6 August, Venus can be found in Virgo, the area of your chart devoted to matters related to far-off places. You could very well form a passion with somebody who comes from abroad, or perhaps somebody who is involved in education. Either way, it looks to be an interesting period.

From 7 August to 7 September, Venus will be in Libra, the area of your chart devoted to work and status. You may be forming relationships – romantic or otherwise – in connection with your job.

From 8 September to the end of the year, Venus will be rooted in Scorpio. This is no bad thing, because it's the area of your chart devoted to your relationships with other people, both on the work front and in your spare time, perhaps as part of a team. New friends with attractive faces enter the scene and you could be positively spoiled for choice. Lucky you, but for heaven's sake don't be your usual conservative self – be prepared to be a little bit more daring, because you will most certainly be glad that you did.

Health and Diet Year

Many people, including myself, are rapidly beginning to recognize the fact that mental attitude can, and does, have a direct effect on physical well-being. Some would argue that 'spiritual health' also plays a large part in maintaining a healthy body and a healthy mind. This is not to suggest that we must live the life of a saint, but nevertheless we should be aware of being on the right path towards our objectives.

It is necessary to be conscious of our beliefs and our goals, otherwise it is quite likely that we may lose our way and then our physical well-being may be undermined by a sense of futility. You know the attitude: 'Is it really worth putting myself out?' 'I try but it doesn't seem to get me anywhere.'

Most of us have experienced these feelings at some time in our lives. Should such an attitude develop, and then be followed by several unfortunate setbacks (which we must all occasionally experience), this can dent our confidence, so that even more serious problems occur if we allow ourselves to be pulled under. Believing we are getting nowhere seems to take all the joy out of life, and certainly undermines our health.

You have an iron constitution, Capricorn, with nerves of steel and tremendous powers of endurance. Your sign rules the knees, and these can cause you trouble from time to time. You may also have problems with the cold, your teeth, broken bones, and perhaps rheumatism later in life. Moods of depression can give rise to chronic over-indulgence. Even so, after Sagittarius this is the best sign for living to a ripe old age.

However, you must admit you tend to worry easily and, therefore, to suffer from stress. The most likely cause of ills for you is your tendency to bottle up your emotions. In fact, all too often you give the impression of being totally unemotional. Your inner sense of propriety and dignity make it hard for you to express your feelings. If, in addition, you were brought up by parents who believed in keeping their feelings under wraps, then this will have laid the foundations for psychosomatic illnesses later on, which can result in nervous problems. It is the utmost importance, therefore, that you learn how to release stress.

Most Goats possess an innate sense of timing. However, this is often rather slower than other people would like, and when you are being harassed or cajoled, tensions build. As a Saturn-ruled sign, it's essential that you recognize this and make those closest to you understand that you do things in your own good time. You are often successful when others have tired themselves out pushing ahead too quickly. It is for this reason that you rarely suffer from the feverish conditions which can haunt the most energetic types.

Routine and practical work provide you with a sense of security, much sought after by those born under Capricorn. However, you have a tendency to become dogmatic and too conscientious. Your attitude may be quite inflexible, and a rigid mind can lead to a rigid body. In order to avoid restriction of movement, you must learn to develop tolerance and flexibility and not to take everything too much to heart. As regards exercise, you should take up anything which keeps you supple. Swimming is perhaps your best method of keeping fit, whereas any sport where the joints can be easily damaged is best avoided.

As for your diet, you need plenty of dairy products, citrus fruits, nuts, bran and yoghurt to remain healthy. Like your opposite sign of Cancer, you should never try to eat when you are upset.

Remember that feelings which are controlled to freezing point can affect the movement of the limbs. Tension is often indicated by the way that limbs are held, and ultimately movement becomes restricted. All of this is avoidable if you're willing to follow at least some of the advice given here.

So how is your health likely to fare this year?

During the first three days of January, Mercury will be in your sign, so it's not surprising that you may be feeling a little bit jittery, possibly because you have over-indulged like crazy (what else can you really expect?).

From 4 January to 3 February and again from 14 February to 11 March, Mercury will be in Aquarius, so if there's anything wrong with you it's likely to be because you are fretting about funds or financial budgets. Do try to keep a sense of proportion and you will have nothing to fear during this time. This is, of course, entirely up to you. Between 4 and 13 February, Mercury moves back into your own sign of Capricorn. This gives you a rather unsettled few days, until Mercury returns to Aquarius.

From 12 March to 12 April, Mercury will be in Aries, the area of your chart devoted to the health of your family. It looks as if you're going to be hale and hearty enough, but someone at home may be feeling a little bit fragile, or perhaps under the weather. Take them to the doctor and then try to put them on a course of vitamins to help build them up.

♑

From 13 to 29 April, Mercury will be in the earthy sign of Taurus. This could prove to be a lively time, with creative and sporting activities to the fore. You might also be in the mood for partying – and there is the possibility of romance in the air.

From 30 April to 6 July, Mercury will be in Gemini. Again you seem to be suffering from a lack of sleep, and picking up minor bugs. The best thing you can do to help yourself is to stay away from those who are laden down with germs, because you really don't want to be laid low at such an important time.

From 7 to 21 July, Mercury will be in Cancer, your opposite sign. It's not surprising that the stars seem to be leeching your energy, enthusiasm and positive thinking. Do your best to shake this off and treat yourself from time to time. This might just help.

From 22 July to 5 August, Mercury will visit the fiery sign of Leo. This may be a time when you have to concentrate on financial issues, and you could be receiving documents or papers from your bank, or meeting up with people you are involved with financially. Don't worry – things will be all right as long as you pay attention to detail.

From 6 to 26 August, Mercury will be in your own sign again. You're going to have the jitters from time to time. Also it would be a good idea to protect yourself from people who are laden down with cold germs, because you will pick things up rather easily.

From 27 August to 1 October, Mercury seems reluctant to leave the sign of Libra, which is not surprising because you are an ambitious sort of person and that's where all of your energy is going – although, of course, from time to time you will be paying a price for this, so do try to develop a sense of proportion, won't you?

From 2 to 10 October, Mercury will be residing in the earthy sign of Virgo. There will be a lot of activity involving children over these few days, whether they are your own, or those of friends and relations. It is possible you may have to pay an unexpected school visit!

On 11 October, Mercury moves on into the airy sign of Libra, where it stays until the end of the month. This is the zenith point of your chart, and the stars indicate that legal matters will become prominent. Also, travel connected with work is well favoured.

On 1 November Mercury will be passing through Scorpio until the 18th, in the area of your chart relating to dealing with other people. Because there is such an upbeat feel at the moment, it's quite likely you'll be partying and going out to pubs or clubs. This is also a good time to study; you will pick new things up really quickly. Won't you be pleased with yourself!

From 19 November to 8 December, Mercury is in Sagittarius, the position in your chart where you could very well play your own worst enemy. Believing, as you do, that you are stronger and more resilient than anybody else, one day Capricorn you're going to wake up to the fact that you are no different from the rest of us, and then you will grow up quite considerably.

Lastly, from 9 December to the end of the year Mercury will be in your own sign. You'll be rushing hither and thither without any clear idea of what you're doing, and this will only stress you out. As a Capricorn, you're very good at taking life a step at a time. Make sure that you apply this method of progress until the end of the year. If you do, you should be able to remain as healthy and as fit as you usually are.

♑

Numerology Year

In order to discover the number of any year you are interested in, your 'individual year number', first take your birth date, day and month, and add this to the year you are interested in, be it in the past or in the future. As an example, say you were born on 13 August and the year you are interested in is 2002:

$$
\begin{array}{r}
13 \\
+ \quad 8 \\
+ \quad 2002 \\
\hline
2023
\end{array}
$$

Then, write down 2 + 0 + 2 + 3 and you will discover this equals 7. This means that your year number is 7. If the number adds up to more than 9, add these two digits together.

You can experiment with this method by taking any year from your past and following this guide to find whether or not numerology works out for you.

The guide is perennial and applicable to all Sun signs: you can look up years for your friends as well as for yourself. Use it to discover general trends ahead, the way you should be

approaching a chosen period and how you can make the most
of the future.

Individual Year Number 1

General Feel
A time for being more self-sufficient and one when you should
be ready to really go for it. All opportunities must be snapped
up, after careful consideration. Also an excellent time for
laying down the foundations for future success in all areas.

Definition
Because this is the number 1 individual year, you will have the
chance to start again in many areas of life. The emphasis will
be upon the new; there will be fresh faces in your life, more
opportunities and perhaps even new experiences. If you were
born on either the 1st, 19th or 28th and were born under the
sign of Aries or Leo then this will be an extremely important
time. It is crucial during this cycle that you be prepared to go
it alone, push back horizons and generally open up your
mind. Time also for playing the leader or pioneer wherever
necessary. If you have a hobby which you wish to turn into
a business, or maybe you simply wish to introduce other
people to your ideas and plans, then do so whilst experiencing
this individual cycle. A great period too for laying down
plans for long-term future gains. Therefore, make sure you
do your homework well and you will reap the rewards at a
later date.

Relationships
This is an ideal period for forming new bonds, perhaps business relationships, new friends and new loves too. You will be

attracted to those in high positions and with strong personalities. There may also be an emphasis on bonding with people a good deal younger than yourself. If you are already in a long-standing relationship, then it is time to clear away the dead wood between you which may have been causing misunderstandings and unhappiness. Whether in love or business, you will find those who are born under the sign of Aries, Leo or Aquarius far more common in your life, also those born on the following dates: 1st, 4th, 9th, 10th, 13th, 18th, 19th, 22nd and 28th. The most important months for this individual year, when you are likely to meet up with those who have a strong influence on you, are January, May, July and October.

Career

It is likely that you have been wanting to break free and to explore fresh horizons in your career and this is definitely a year for doing so. Because you are in a fighting mood, and because your decision-making qualities as well as your leadership qualities are foremost, it will be an easy matter for you to find assistance as well as to impress other people. Major professional changes are likely and you will also feel more independent within your existing job. Should you want times for making important career moves, then choose Mondays or Tuesdays. These are good days for pushing your luck and presenting your ideas well. Changes connected with your career are going to be more likely during April, May, July and September.

Health

If you have forgotten the name of your doctor or dentist, then this is the year to start regular checkups. A time too when people of a certain age are likely to start wearing glasses. The emphasis seems to be on the eyes. Start a good health regime. This will help you cope with any adverse events that almost assuredly lie ahead. The important months for your own health as well as for loved ones are March, May and August.

Individual Year Number 2

General Feel
You will find it far easier to relate to other people.

Definition
What you will need during this cycle is diplomacy, cooperation and the ability to put yourself in someone else's shoes. Whatever you began last year will now begin to show signs of progress. However, don't expect miracles; changes are going to be slow rather than at the speed of light. Changes will be taking place all around you. It is possible too that you will be considering moving from one area to another, maybe even to another country. There is a lively feel about domesticity and in relationships with the opposite sex too. This is going to be a marvellous year for making things come true and asking for favours. However, on no account should you force yourself and your opinions on other people. A spoonful of honey is going to get you a good deal further than a spoonful of vinegar. If you are born under the sign of Cancer or Taurus, or if your birthday falls on the 2nd, 11th, 20th or 29th, then this year is going to be full of major events.

Relationships
You need to associate with other people far more than is usually the case – perhaps out of necessity. The emphasis is on love, friendship and professional partnerships. The opposite

sex will be much more prepared to get involved in your life than is normally the case. This year you have a far greater chance of becoming engaged or married, and there is likely to be a lovely addition both to your family and to the families of your friends and those closest to you. The instinctive and caring side to your personality is going to be strong and very obvious. You will quickly discover that you will be particularly touchy and sensitive to things that other people say. Further, you will find those born under the sign of Cancer, Taurus and Libra entering your life far more than is usually the case. This also applies to those who are born on the 2nd, 6th, 7th, 11th, 15th, 20th, 24th, 25th or 29th of the month.

Romantic and family events are likely to be emphasized during April, June and September.

Career

There is a strong theme of change here, but there is no point in having a panic attack about that because, after all, life is about change. However, in this particular individual year any transformation or upheaval is likely to be of an internal nature, such as at your place of work, rather than external. You may find your company is moving from one area to another, or perhaps there are changes between departments. Quite obviously then, the most important thing for you to do in order to make your life easy is to be adaptable. There is a strong possibility too that you may be given added responsibility. Do not flinch as this will bring in extra reward.

If you are thinking of searching for employment this year, then try to arrange all meetings and negotiations on Monday and Friday. These are good days for asking for favours or rises too. The best months are March, April, June, August, and December. All these are important times for change.

β

Health

This individual cycle emphasizes stomach problems. The
important thing for you is to eat sensibly, rather than go on a
crash diet, for example – this could be detrimental. If you are
female then you would be wise to have a checkup at least
once during the year ahead just to be sure you can continue to
enjoy good health. All should be discriminating when dining
out. Check cutlery, and take care that food has not been par-
tially cooked. Furthermore, emotional stress could get you
down, but only if you allow it. Provided you set aside some
periods of relaxation in each day when you can close your
eyes and let everything drift away, you will have little to
worry about. When it comes to diet, be sure that the emphasis
is on nutrition, rather than fighting the flab. Perhaps it would
be a good idea to become less weight conscious during this
period and let your body find its natural ideal weight on its
own. The months of February, April, July and November may
show health changes in some way. Common sense is your
best guide during this year.

Individual Year Number 3

General Feel

You are going to be at your most creative and imaginative
during this time. There is a theme of expansion and growth
and you will want to polish up your self-image in order to
make the 'big impression'.

Definition

It is a good year for reaching out, for expansion. Social and
artistic developments should be interesting as well as profitable and this will help to promote happiness. There will be a

strong urge in you to improve yourself – either your image or your reputation or, perhaps, your mind. Your popularity soars through the ceiling and this delights you. Involving yourself with something creative brings increased success plus a good deal of satisfaction. However, it is imperative that you keep yourself in a positive mood. This will attract attention and appreciation of all your talents. Projects which were begun two years ago are likely to be bearing fruit this year. If you are born under the sign of Pisces or Sagittarius, or your birthday falls on the 3rd, 12th, 21st or 30th, then this year is going to be particularly special and successful.

Relationships

There is a happy-go-lucky feel about all your relationships and you are in a flirty, fancy-free mood. Heaven help anyone trying to catch you during the next twelve months: they will need to get their skates on. Relationships are likely to be light-hearted and fun rather than heavy going. It is possible too that you will find yourself with those who are younger than you, particularly those born under the signs of Pisces and Sagittarius, and those whose birth dates add up to 3, 6 or 9. Your individual cycle shows important months for relationships are March, May, August and December.

Career

As I discussed earlier, this individual number is one that suggests branching out and personal growth, so be ready to take on anything new. Not surprisingly, your career prospects look bright and shiny. You are definitely going to be more ambitious and must keep up that positive façade and attract opportunities. Avoid taking obligations too lightly; it is important that you adopt a conscientious approach to all your responsibilities. You may take on a fresh course of learning or look for a new job, and the important days for doing so would be on Thursday and Friday: these are definitely your best days. This is particularly true in the months of February, March, May, July and November: expect expansion in your life and take a chance during these times.

Health

Because you are likely to be out and about painting the town all the colours of the rainbow, it is likely that health problems could come through over-indulgence or perhaps tiredness. However, if you must have some health problems, I suppose these are the best ones to experience, because they are under your control. There is also a possibility that you may get a little fraught over work, which may result in some emotional scenes. However, you are sensible enough to realize they should not be taken too seriously. If you are prone to skin allergies, then these too could be giving you problems during this particular year. The best advice you can follow is not to go to extremes that will affect your body or your mind. It is all very well to have fun, but after a while too much of it affects not only your health but also the degree of enjoyment you experience. Take extra care between January and March, and June and October, especially where these are winter months for you.

Individual Year Number 4

General Feel

It is back to basics this year. Do not build on shaky foundations. Get yourself organized and be prepared to work a little harder than you usually do and you will come through without any great difficulty.

Definition

It is imperative that you have a grand plan. Do not simply rush off without considering the consequences and avoid dabbling of any kind. It is likely too that you will be gathering more responsibility and on occasions this could lead you to feeling unappreciated, claustrophobic and perhaps over-burdened in some ways. Although it is true to say that this cycle in your individual life tends to bring about a certain amount of limitation, whether this be on the personal, the psychological or the financial side of life, you now have the chance to get yourself together and to build on more solid foundations. Security is definitely your key word at this time. When it comes to any project, job or plan, it is important that you ask the right questions. In other words, do your homework and do not rush blindly into anything. That would be a disaster. If you are an Aquarius, a Leo or a Gemini or you are born on the 4th, 13th, 22nd, or the 31st of any month, this individual year will be extremely important and long remembered.

Relationships

You will find that it is the eccentric, the unusual, the unconventional and the downright odd that will be drawn into your life during this particular cycle. It is also strongly possible that people you have not met for some time may be re-entering your circle and an older person or somebody outside your own social or perhaps religious background will be drawn to you too. When it comes to the romantic side of life, again you are drawn to that which is different from usual. You may even form a relationship with someone who comes from a totally different background, perhaps from far away. Something unusual about them stimulates and excites you. Gemini, Leo and Aquarius are your likely favourites, as well as anyone whose birth number adds up to 1, 4, 5 or 7. Certainly the most exciting months for romance are going to be February, April, July and November. Make sure then that you socialize a lot during these particular times, and be ready for literally anything.

Career

Once more we have the theme of the unusual and different in this area of life. You may be plodding along in the same old rut when suddenly lightning strikes and you find yourself besieged by offers from other people and, in a panic, not quite sure what to do. There may be a period when nothing particular seems to be going on when, to your astonishment, you are given a promotion or some exciting challenge. Literally anything can happen in this particular cycle of your life. The individual year 4 also inclines towards added responsibilities and it is important that you do not off-load them onto other people or cringe in fear. They will eventually pay off and in the meantime you will be gaining in experience and paving the way for greater success in the future. When you want to arrange any kind of meeting, negotiation or perhaps ask for a favour at work, then try to do so on a Monday or a Wednesday for the luckiest results. January, February, April, October and November are certainly the months when you must play the opportunist and be ready to say yes to anything that comes your way.

Health

The biggest problems that you will have to face this year are caused by stress, so it is important that you attend to your diet and take life as philosophically as possible, as well as being ready to adapt to changing conditions. You are likely to find that people you thought you knew well are acting out of character and this throws you off balance. Take care, too, when visiting the doctor. Remember that you are dealing with a human being and that doctors, like the rest of us, can make mistakes. Unless you are 100 per cent satisfied then go for a second opinion over anything important. Try to be sceptical about yourself because you are going to be a good deal more moody than usual. The times that need special attention are February, May, September and November. If any of these months fall in the winter part of your year, then wrap up well and dose up on vitamin C.

Individual Year Number 5

General Feel
There will be many more opportunities for you to get out and about, and travel is certainly going to be playing a large part in your year. Change, too, must be expected and even embraced – after all, it is part of life. You will have more free time and choices, so all in all things look promising.

Definition
It is possible that you tried previously to get something off the launchpad, but for one reason or another it simply didn't happen. Luckily, you now get a chance to renew those old plans and put them into action. You are certainly going to feel that things are changing for the better in all areas. You will be more actively involved with the public and enjoy a certain amount of attention and publicity. You may have failed in the past but this year mistakes will be easier to accept and learn from; you are going to find yourself both physically and men- tally more in tune with your environment and with those you

care about than ever before. If you are a Gemini or a Virgo or are born on the 5th, 14th or 23rd, then this is going to be a period of major importance for you and you must be ready to take advantage of this.

Relationships

Lucky you! Your sexual magnetism goes through the ceiling and you will be involved in many relationships during the year ahead. You have that extra charisma about you which will be attracting others and you can look forward to being choosy. There will be an inclination to be drawn to those who are considerably younger than yourself. It is likely too that you will find that those born under the signs of Taurus, Gemini, Virgo and Libra as well as those whose birth date adds up to 2, 5 or 6 will play an important part in your year. The months for attracting others in a big way are January, March, June, October and December.

Career

This is considered by all numerologists as being one of the best numbers for self-improvement in all areas, but particularly on the professional front. It will be relatively easy for you to sell your ideas and yourself, as well as to push your skills and expertise under the noses of other people. They will certainly sit up and take notice. Clearly, then, this is a time for you to view the world as your oyster and to get out there and grab your piece of the action. You have increased confidence and should be able to get exactly what you want. Friday and Wednesday are perhaps the best days if looking for a job or going to negotiations or interviews, or in fact for generally pushing yourself into the limelight. Watch out for March, May, September, October or December. Something of great importance could pop up at this time. There will certainly be a chance for advancement; whether you take it or not is, of course, entirely up to you.

Health

Getting a good night's rest could be your problem during the year ahead, since that mind of yours is positively buzzing and won't let you rest. Try turning your brain off at bedtime, otherwise you will finish up irritable and exhausted. Try to take things a step at a time without rushing around. Meditation may help you to relax and do more for your physical well-being than anything else. Because this is an extremely active year, you will need to do some careful planning so that you can cope with ease rather than rushing around like a demented mayfly. Furthermore, try to avoid going over the top with alcohol, food, sex, gambling or anything which could be described as a 'quick fix'. During January, April, August and October, watch yourself a bit, you could do with some pampering, particularly if these happen to be winter months for you.

Individual Year Number 6

General Feel

There is likely to be increased responsibility and activity within your domestic life. There will be many occasions when you will be helping loved ones and your sense of duty is going to be strong.

Definition

Activities for the most part are likely to be centred around property, family, loved ones, romance and your home. Your artistic appreciation will be good and you will be drawn to

anything that is colourful and beautiful, and possessions that
have a strong appeal to your eye or even your ear. Where
domesticity is concerned, there is a strong suggestion that you
may move out of one home into another. This is an excellent
time, too, for self-education, for branching out, for graduat-
ing, for taking on some extra courses – whether simply to
improve your appearance or to improve your mind. When it
comes to your social life you are inundated with chances to
attend events. You are going to be a real social butterfly, flit-
ting from scene to scene and enjoying yourself thoroughly.
Try to accept nine out of ten invitations that come your way
because they bring with them chances of advancement. If you
are born on the 6th, 15th or 24th, or should your birth sign be
Taurus, Libra or Cancer, then this year will be long remembered as a very positive one.

Relationships

When it comes to love, sex and romance the individual year 6
is perhaps the most successful. It is a time for being swept off
your feet, for becoming engaged or even getting married. On
the more negative side, perhaps, there could be separation
and divorce. However, the latter can be avoided, provided
you are prepared to sit down and communicate properly.
There is an emphasis too on pregnancy and birth, or changes
in existing relationships. Circumstances will be sweeping you
along. If you are born under the sign of Taurus, Cancer or
Libra, then it is even more likely that this will be a major year
for you, as well as for those born on dates adding up to 6, 3 or
2. The most memorable months of your year are going to be
February, May, September and November. Grab all opportunities to enjoy yourself and improve your relationships
during these periods.

Career

A good year for this side of life too, with the chances of promotion and recognition for past efforts all coming your way. You will be able to improve your position in life even though it is likely that recently you have been disappointed. On the cash front, big rewards will come flooding in mainly because you are prepared to fulfil your obligations and commitments without complaint or protest. Other people will appreciate all the efforts you have put in, so plod along and you will find your efforts will not have been in vain. Perversely, if you are looking for a job or setting up an interview, negotiation or a meeting, or simply want to advertise your talents in some way, then your best days for doing so are Monday, Thursday and Friday. Long-term opportunities are very strong during the months of February, April, August, September and November. These are the key periods for pushing yourself up the ladder of success.

Health

If you are to experience any problems of a physical nature during this year, then they could be tied up with the throat, nose or the tonsils, plus the upper parts of the body. Basically, what you need to stay healthy during this year is plenty of sunlight, moderate exercise, fresh air and changes of scene. Escape to the coast if this is at all possible. The months for being particularly watchful are March, July, September and December. Think twice before doing anything during these times and there is no reason why you shouldn't stay hale and hearty for the whole year.

Individual Year Number 7

General Feel

A year for inner growth and for finding out what really makes you tick and what you need to make you happy. Self-awareness and discovery are all emphasized during the individual year 7.

Definition

You will be provided with the opportunity to place as much emphasis as possible on your personal life and your own well-being. There will be many occasions when you will find yourself analysing your past motives and actions, and giving more attention to your own personal needs, goals and desires. There will also be many occasions when you will want to escape any kind of confusion, muddle or noise; time spent alone will not be wasted. This will give you the chance to meditate and also to examine exactly where you have come to so far, and where you want to go in the future. It is important you make up your mind what you want out of this particular year because once you have done so you will attain those ambitions. Failure to do this could mean you end up chasing your own tail and that is a pure waste of time and energy. You will also discover that secrets about yourself and other people could be surfacing during this year. If you are born under the sign of Pisces or Cancer, or on the 7th, 16th or 25th of the month, then this year will be especially wonderful.

Relationships

It has to be said from the word go that this is not the best year for romantic interest. A strong need for contemplation will mean spending time on your own. Any romance that does develop this year may not live up to your expectations, but,

providing you are prepared to take things as they come without jumping to conclusions, then you will enjoy yourself
without getting hurt. Decide exactly what it is you have in
mind and then go for it. Romantic interests this year are likely
to be with people who are born on dates that add up to 2, 4 or
7, or with people born under the sign of Cancer or Pisces.
Watch for romantic opportunities during January, April,
August and October.

Career

When we pass through this particular individual cycle, two
things in life tend to occur: retirement from the limelight, and
a general slowing down, perhaps by taking leave of absence
or maybe retraining in some way. It is likely too that you will
become more aware of your own occupational expertise and
skills – you will begin to understand your true purpose in life
and will feel much more enlightened. Long-sought-after goals
begin to come to life if you have been drifting of late. The best
attitude to have throughout this year is an exploratory one
when it comes to your work. If you want to set up negotiations, interviews or meetings, arrange them for Monday or
Friday. In fact, any favours you seek should be tackled on
these days. January, March, July, August, October and
December are particularly good for self-advancement.

Health

Since, in comparison to previous years, this is a rather quiet
time, health problems are likely to be minor. Some will possibly
come through irritation or worry and the best thing to do is to
attempt to remain meditative and calm. This state of mind will
bring positive results. Failure to do so may create unnecessary
problems by allowing your imagination to run completely out

of control. You need time this year to restore, recuperate and contemplate. Any health changes that do occur are likely to happen in February, June, August and November.

Individual Year Number 8

General Feel

This is going to be a time for success, for making important moves and changes, a time when you may gain power and certainly one when your talents are going to be recognized.

Definition

This individual year gives you the chance to 'think big'; it is a time when you can occupy the limelight and wield power. If you were born on the 8th, 17th or 26th of the month or come under the sign of Capricorn, pay attention to this year and make sure you make the most of it. You should develop greater maturity and discover a true feeling of faith and destiny, both in yourself and in events that occur. This part of the cycle is connected with career, ambition and money, but debts from the past will have to be repaid. For example, an old responsibility or debt that you may have avoided in past years may reappear to haunt you. However, whatever you do with these twelve months, aim high – think big, think success and above all be positive.

Relationships

This particular individual year is one which is strongly connected with birth, divorce and marriage – most of the land-marks we experience in life, in fact. Love-wise, those who are more experienced or older than you, or people of power, authority, influence or wealth, will be very attractive. This year will be putting you back in touch with those from your past – old friends, comrades, associates, and even romances from long ago crop up once more. You should not experience any great problems romantically this year, especially if you are dealing with Capricorns or Librans, or with those whose date of birth adds up to 8, 6 or 3. The best months for romance to develop are likely to be March, July, September and December.

Career

The number 8 year is generally believed to be the best one when it comes to bringing in cash. It is also good for asking for a rise or achieving promotion or authority over other people. This is your year for basking in the limelight of success, the result perhaps of your past efforts. Now you will be rewarded. Financial success is all but guaranteed, provided you keep faith with your ambitions and yourself. It is important that you set major goals for yourself and work slowly towards them. You will be surprised how easily they are fulfilled. Conversely, if you are looking for work, then do set up interviews, negotiations and meetings, preferably on Saturday, Thursday or Friday, which are your luckiest days. Also watch out for chances to do yourself a bit of good during February, June, July, September and November.

Health

You can avoid most health problems, particularly headaches, constipation or liver problems, by avoiding depression and feelings of loneliness. It is important when these descend that you keep yourself busy enough not to dwell on them. When it comes to receiving attention from the medical profession you would be well advised to get a second opinion. Eat wisely, try to

keep a positive and enthusiastic outlook on life and all will be
well. Periods which need special care are January, May, July and
October. Therefore, if these months fall during the winter part of
your year, wrap up well and dose yourself with vitamins.

Individual Year Number 9

General Feel
A time for tying up loose ends. Wishes are likely to be fulfilled
and matters brought to swift conclusions. Inspiration runs
amok. Much travel is likely.

Definition
The number 9 individual year is perhaps the most successful
of all. It tends to represent the completion of matters and
affairs, whether in work, business, or personal affairs. Your
ability to let go of habits, people and negative circumstances
or situations, that may have been holding you back, is strong.
The sympathetic and humane side to your character also sur-
faces and you learn to give more freely of yourself without
expecting anything in return. Any good deeds that you do
will certainly be well rewarded in terms of satisfaction, and
perhaps financially, too. If you are born under the sign of
Aries or Scorpio, or on the 9th, 18th or 27th of the month, this
is certainly going to be an all-important year.

Relationships
The individual year 9 is a cycle which gives appeal as well as
influence. Because of this, you will be getting emotionally tied
up with members of the opposite sex who may be outside
your usual cultural or ethnic group. The reason for this is that
this particular number relates to humanity and of course this

tends to quash ignorance, pride and bigotry. You also discover that Aries, Leo and Scorpio people are going to be much more evident in your domestic affairs, as well as those whose birth dates add up to 9, 3 or 1. The important months for relationships are February, June, August and November. These will be extremely hectic and eventful from a romantic viewpoint and there are times when you could be swept off your feet.

Career

This is a year which will help to make many of your dreams and ambitions come true. Furthermore, it is an excellent time for success if you are involved in marketing your skills, talents and expertise more widely. You may be thinking of expanding abroad for example and, if so, this is certainly a good idea. You will find that harmony and cooperation with your fellow workers are easier than before and this will help your dreams and ambitions. The best days for you if you want to line up meetings or negotiations are going to be Tuesdays and Thursdays, and this also applies if you are looking for employment or want a special day for doing something of an ambitious nature. Employment or business changes could also feature during January, May, June, August and October.

Health

The only physical problems you may have during this particular year will be because of accidents, so be careful. Try, too, to avoid unnecessary tension and arguments with other people. Take extra care when you are on the roads: no drinking and driving, for example. You will only have problems if you play your own worst enemy. Be extra careful when in the kitchen or bathroom: sharp instruments that you find in these areas can lead to cuts, unless you take care.

Your Sun Sign Partner

Capricorn with Capricorn

This is more of a primitive power struggle than a starry-eyed romance. In the better moments you can understand where the other person is coming from, but it's another thing trying to tolerate it.

Basically, you both want to be boss and possess an unquestionable assurance that your way is the right way. In such a conflict it is difficult for either of you to concede. Therefore, there comes a time for mutual scowling and sulking.

All Capricorns need to learn how to cavort with life and to be less cautious, so a steady but blithe spirit would bring you a lot more sunshine. When Capricorns learn that they haven't forgotten how to love, out comes the sharpest sense of humour.

Capricorn Woman

Capricorn woman with Aries man
On the surface she is cool and steady, but on all levels he is a crazed madman who means well. Therefore, he'll be enthralled by the way she carves her way to greatness.

She will be a little overwhelmed as he comes dashing into her life and knocks her door off its hinges. She'll think he's nice but maybe from another planet when he moves about the living room like a Mexican jumping bean, and in the middle of a conversation starts doing push-ups.

If he wants a woman who is real, then she is for him. However, if he is more interested in pursuing a challenge than giving of himself, she should go elsewhere. She has no tolerance for little boys who try to make the world believe they are men. She's too sensitive to live with a facade, while sometimes he is insensitive enough to prefer one.

Capricorn woman with Taurus man

She'll find him better than a Christmas present on a cold, rainy morning. He'll find her to be the kind of competent career woman he's always had a crush on.

She is strong and dignified, yet has a lot of feeling under a cool surface. He is warm and cuddly with an earthiness that makes her feel at ease.

She will inspire his career goals, while he'll make her feel loved for herself rather than her status. Her encouragement will help him to drive himself to greater places. His measured pace will help her to slow down and live longer. These two will develop a glow and a tenderness and they'll be quite happy to announce their love to the world at large.

Capricorn woman with Gemini man

This is definitely not a match made in heaven. Neither party can really understand where the other person is coming from, but even if someone told her, it wouldn't be of much help. She needs reassurance in a relationship, but the only kind that he can give her is that he is the one person she'll never get it from. He heartily enjoys frolicking from one woman to another, while she is capable of sitting still if there is something to sit for.

At best this can be a friendship, at the very worst it can be a marriage. In general she is too sane, stable and successful for his tastes. He needs a woman who, after he torments her with a grin, will still look up to him because he is so witty. However, after a few of his choice performances the Capricorn woman will give him the cold shoulder and will tell him that what's really amusing is that one day his capricious antics will make him very sad.

Capricorn woman with Cancer man

She'll be touched by the way he seems to care for her welfare. But she'll have a hard time taking on his moods. He seems to invent slights and then sulk about them. And no matter what she does, she can never discover what she said wrong.

He'll wonder why she spends so much time at the office. In turn, she'll resent his suspicions and the way he makes her feel guilty. If she can look at him from a less superficial standpoint, she may find a man who is very much worthy of her attentions. However, the price she has to pay for his sympathy and services is some of her own. The more she lets what happened at the afternoon's board meeting get in the way of their better moments, the more she will be prying apart a potentially happy union.

Capricorn woman with Leo man

He'll meet her at a tennis club. She won't be playing, only watching, but her outfit will be more smashing than his backhand.

To all appearances she has class. If she didn't originally have it, she's paid a lot to get it, and she's seeking a reward, the bigger the better. She's guaranteed to love him the moment she sees him put down a large sum of money. And to keep her eyelashes a-flutter, he'll keep producing more, even if he has to excuse himself politely to do a little counterfeiting.

She is serious, supportive, faithful and trusting. She is also usually successful. Her credit will exalt him, and her concern will overwhelm him. If he gives her enough Leo love, she might even forget she wanted a fur coat.

Capricorn woman with Virgo man

Since neither of these two knows how to sit still, they'll indulge each other's tendency to workaholism. He will applaud the discipline, tenacity and drive that will take her straight to the top. She in turn will approve of his Sundays spent at the office to make his projects perfect. She will be touched by his shyness and impressed by his strong resolve. He has the discipline to get up at 6 a.m. to take a self-improvement course. That's because every day, in every way, he somehow tries to be a little better.

She likes a man who has his life under control. He likes a woman with drive and ambition. Together, they could have great rapport and compatibility. This is a marriage that could last a lifetime.

Capricorn woman with Libra man

Any way she looks at it, he is not as intense as she is. While she sits back and smoulders with quiet zeal, he analyses what he should be feeling. She appreciates his approach to aesthetics, but when she just wants someone to grab her, he generates as much heat as an air conditioner.

It takes him half an hour to order three courses on a menu, while she makes up her mind with just one glance. He lets his insecurities overwhelm him, while she keeps hers coolly under cover.

However, when she needs a shoulder to cry on she'll have to look elsewhere, because he'll probably be too distressed over some trivial problem of his own. He is the kind of man who is ethereal, fickle and self-indulgent. If he overcomes these traits and decides to dwell in his higher being, this relationship could become a close one. If not, consider it another rhapsody in blue.

Capricorn woman with Scorpio man

In this relationship there's a lot of talk and very little emotional understanding. However, in many ways the attraction is so irresistible that it borders on being fatal. From the very start, she'll be bewitched and he'll be feverish. The ensuing situation could be definitely erotic, but in the long run an emotional dead end.

He has a hard time accepting her as she is, because he feels he doesn't really deserve her. Therefore, he loves the idea of her, but the actuality makes him nervous and he may try to restrict the relationship to brief encounters. In the main, this wouldn't be a bad idea.

Capricorn woman with Sagittarius man

His attitude is 'don't worry'. Hers is, 'if I don't worry about it, nobody else will'.

Basically, these two are going in opposite directions. She will appreciate the way he makes her chuckle after a dreary day. However, since she also expects some sophisticated and dignified behaviour, she'll be grievously disappointed. He's truly taken in by her warmth, but he'll probably decide it's too much of a strain to try to make her feel satisfied and womanly. Since he spreads his love so thin, the chances are that he will never take her seriously.

Capricorn woman with Aquarius man

He's a bit more unconventional than she could ever imagine. And more freedom-loving than she may feel comfortable with. However, because he is more fun than a circus, he may make her lose some of her Capricorn control.

Mr Aquarius is quite impervious to considerations of the present, since his mind likes to dwell in the future. She, on the other hand, prefers to live in the here and now.

If she can put up with his physical passivity and doesn't mind taking total charge of his life and all its menial details, then this could very well become a happy relationship or a marriage. It may expand her earthy mind and cure her of her persistent melancholia. In turn she may ground his eccentric ideas and help him make them materialize.

Capricorn woman with Pisces man

At first he will seem romantic and sentimental, at second glance, weak and wishy-washy. He has a hard time dealing with the day-to-day world, while she thrives in competitive places.

His mind is floating somewhere over the clouds, whereas hers is rooted firmly on earth. She is a no-nonsense person who doesn't have time for adolescent instability in an adult whose hair is turning grey. Her attitude is, 'Either shape up or ship out.' His is, 'Take me or leave me, but just don't bug me.'

Any way you look at it, his way is not her way, unless she likes a lot of giving and very little getting.

Capricorn Man

Capricorn man with Aries woman

He'll worry that she works so hard that she'll destroy her health. She will angrily reply that he is being over-cautious. Deep down, he is a good soul who means well, but she may at times find him gloomy.

If he makes a commitment to her, she will remain uppermost in his mind and he will never try to avoid what he feels he has to do. However, he is controlling, chauvinistic and embraces a double standard that she may have to break down before she goes any further. He has advice to offer on every subject, which she might find somewhat irritating, since she is not used to listening to unsolicited opinions.

However, if both relinquish their individual need to supervise and control, and instead put their energies into trying to understand each other, this relationship could take them any place they might want to go. Just keep in mind that it's not the fights that matter, but the making up.

Capricorn man with Taurus woman

He is the archetypal ambitious breadwinner, and the kind of man she would like to take command of her life. She is the fertile earth mother, and the kind of woman he would like to serve.

Both share a sense of practicality and purpose that will draw them together. He is responsible, dutiful, loyal and loving. She is solid, stable, devoted and nurturing.

She admires his ambitious, hard-working nature. He respects her resourcefulness and understands her need for security. Together they could build a business, a marriage, a family or a corporation.

♑

Capricorn man with Gemini woman

She'll think him a bore because he would rather work than go dancing. He'll think that she should be locked up when he sees the scattered way she runs her life. She is wilful and defiant; he is commanding and bossy. He can dedicate his life to one sense of purpose, where she has no idea what that means, since she changes her mind every other minute.

She'll make him feel uneasy, since he's never met anyone quite so crazy. He may find her so foreign to his sensibilities that he may ask her to marry him because he thinks her more entertaining than going to the cinema. Now, he is not exactly her definition of mind-shattering excitement, but he is warm, supportive, sincere and willing to put up with all her insane behaviour. Besides loving her, he is the man to help her to get her life together and give her a lot more than she could ever think to ask for.

Capricorn man with Cancer woman

He is the security she's always longed for; she is the woman who can give him the warmth he so needs. Between these two there's an undeniable attraction and a very basic understanding.

Basically, she needs a strong man she can care for, while he needs a woman who knows how to care. Her vulnerable femininity will melt his cool veneer, and his competence and ambition will win her highest respect.

Together they can live a cozy life, showering lots of love on each other and sharing many close moments. Within the depths of her heart he'll be able to see the same insecurities that bring on his own melancholy moments.

Capricorn man with Leo woman

He takes life seriously, so if she really wants him she'll have to keep her temper in check and tread lightly. If she smiles sweetly and speaks softly, he'll walk the dog and take out the rubbish, and forget there are other women in the world.

His price for such supreme fidelity is control. Like Mr Leo, he loves telling women what to do at every waking moment. He was probably the original model for the male chauvinist, and his ideas haven't changed much since the term was coined.

Together they share an appreciation of the very best. He can be a snob, a materialist and an idolater. She views her trinkets as toys, however, while he views his possessions as a measure of his self-worth. She really can't blame him, since he's probably half-killed himself just to get them and they represent the way he drives himself past endurable limits.

Capricorn man with Virgo woman

Even if he's president of five different companies, on the inside he's just a little boy who wants to be taken care of. Because Ms Virgo needs to be needed, appreciated and applauded, this combination could work out well. She'll handle him when he gets bossy, and he in turn will make her life better with his constant care and concern. On dreary days she will cook him a beautiful dinner, and then offer him her critical advice on the problems that seem to him most pressing.

This combination has the makings of great happiness, mutual trust, responsibility and a love that can create a mature kind of marriage.

Capricorn man with Libra woman

Deep down inside, these two are insecure. However, he has a much stronger personality and a tendency to be controlling. At first she may feel it divine to be so loved; however, on second thought she has to admit that he is truly bossy.

He is the tree she can lean on, but the harder she leans, the greater the price. At his most primitive self he is the most outrageous kind of male chauvinist who will tell her what to eat, when to cross the road, and what to cook to keep him happy.

If Ms Libra happens to favour a man who is seeking to transform a free woman into a slave, he is definitely the man for her. What she will get in return for such subjugation is the assurance that he loves her. With a life like this, she'll need all the assurance she can get.

Capricorn man with Scorpio woman

She'll admire his ambition, but get lonely when she never sees him. He respects her devotion, but at times tends to take it for granted. At worst, this union can turn into a bitter and emotional foray; at best it can be a situation of mutual respect, much support and a shared sense of responsibility.

One thing to remember is that she holds the power. Although he may appear to be stern, staunch, overbearing and even critical, she can turn him into molten marshmallow with her warmth, emotional sensitivity and sexual passion. No matter how much he loves her, at times he will feel lonely. She may stay up all night listening to his tales of thwarted ambition, but when she cries her eyes out in his presence he'll inform her that he's going to the store to buy eggs for breakfast.

Once committed, he is faithful, enduring, patient and paternalistic. His inordinate ambition will vicariously bring her the power she so appreciates. But no matter how much she loves him, she may always feel there is something missing.

Capricorn man with Sagittarius woman

On the inside he is as vulnerable as her pet dog, but on the outside he can be unbelievably bossy. He'll tell her what time to go to bed, state that she has no control over her life and imperiously reminds her that he does.

He is dutiful but terribly intolerant, with a will that could easily make her forget that she is a free person. Because, generally speaking, her liberty means more to her than her love life, and so she will be better off to let him try controlling someone else. Greater communication exists between people speaking different languages than between these two.

Capricorn man with Aquarius woman

She is sometimes eccentric and very freedom-loving, while he is insecure. This is where the differences begin; where they end is infinity.

She is a dreamer, while he is a man of the material world. She is fascinated by a multitude of people, but he is more concerned about himself. She is a woman who lives in the future, while he is consumed by matters close at hand. She views life through an unconventional framework, while he holds tightly to tradition. She abandons herself to her mental interests, while he spends time merely making money.

Not only are both coming from different places, they're both wilful enough to try to bring the other along. It won't work. They must either learn to accept each other or both take a walk and look for somebody else.

Capricorn man with Pisces woman

He'll be the father figure she's always been searching for, and she'll be his woman of romance. She needs a strong man she can depend on, and he needs a woman who knows how to need. She'll bolster his ego when she comes running to him for advice and a shoulder to cry on. In turn, he'll tell her what to do and demand that she follow his instructions implicitly.

Emotionally, he'll never understand where she's coming from or where she's going. She cries over things that he couldn't care less about, like sad stories in the news, the problems of people she's never even met, and her own mysterious moods, which seem to him to be silly.

He'll try to introduce her to some practicality; she'll try to introduce him to poetic sensitivity, which he never knew he was capable of. Together, if they are both determined to learn from their differences, they can create a loving relationship that will put them in touch with themselves, as well as with each other.

℔

Monthly and Daily Guides

JANUARY

Until 19 January the Sun will be drifting along in the earthy sign of Capricorn, the area of your chart which rules all of your self-interest. You've more confidence than you know what to do with at this time, so you should push ahead with everything that is important to you.

From 20 January the Sun will be moving into Aquarius, the financial area of your chart. Well, of course, at the best of times you are, shall we say, a little frugal, a little careful with money, but at this time you're not going to be parted from your hard-earned dosh by anyone unless you decide for yourself to do so.

It's a particularly good time for those of you involved in banking and the monetary professions. Use your instincts and you'll be gathering in the garlands for most of this time.

Mercury will be in your own sign for the first few days, so that's a good time for making all kinds of important decisions, as well as signing major paperwork and documents.

On 4 January Mercury will be moving into Aquarius, once more the financial area of your chart. Finances seem to be of prime importance at this time. You might be travelling for the sake of money, possibly interviewing other people you would like to be involved with (because you believe that they could help you, or perhaps it's a mutual thing), but – and it's a big but – remember that Mercury will be in retrograde movement from 18 January to 7 February, and as a result travel, methods of transport and paperwork could hold some kind of danger for you, so do be careful.

Venus is situated in your own sign until mid-month, so you're looking good, feeling good and it's a wonderful time for romance, making commitments, artistic work and perhaps even travel. From 18 January until the end of the month, Venus will be in Aquarius, and so the planets are looking kindly on your financial affairs and those areas connected with possessions. It may be that you receive some belated or unexpected presents, and also some social invitations.

Mars will be in Pisces until 18 January, the area of your chart devoted to the mind. You could be a little bit too impulsive. Furthermore, short journeys could hold a certain amount of danger, so don't drink and drive, and keep your eyes fixed on traffic lights during this period.

From 19 January until the end of the month, Mars will be in Aries, the area of your chart devoted to property and family, parts of your life where there could be some tension and bad feeling and also, perhaps, some mad explosions from time to time. Somebody's going to have to use some common sense, Capricorn, and as you're the one who usually possesses this stuff, it might be a good idea for you to try and bring peace and harmony back to the home once more. It shouldn't be too difficult if you put your mind to it.

The pattern made by the stars during this month supplies a serious concentration of planets in your sign, which may confuse you from time to time, but on the other hand it's going to stop you from being bored. All opportunities that crop up should be seriously considered before you turn them down, because to do so will mean that later on in the year you're going to regret it in a big way, and that would be a great shame.

Furthermore, it is important that you remember that Mars will be in Pisces, the area of your chart devoted to short-distance travel and the mind. You might become impatient, you could be prone to accidents with hot and sharp objects and you may even prang the car, which is most unlike you because, let's face it Capricorn, generally speaking you're an extremely careful person.

January, then, seems to be a bit of a muddle. See what you can do to sort it out, because quite frankly if you can't, then nobody else will be able to help you.

1 TUESDAY Although you're not as close, or at least even friendly, with certain people you still seem to have a good relationship with them. But, no matter how well you know them, you may be astonished by their actions, but still decide to follow them – purely on impulse. You could also choose to opt out and leave at any given moment that you feel like.

2 WEDNESDAY Apart from feeling bad about letting every-one down, you also have a few personal problems of your own. Never mind. The chances are that what takes place over the next few days could leave you deflated, particularly if you were unceremoniously dumped recently. There are also other reasons, but you must keep these to yourself for the time being.

3 THURSDAY It seems that some kind of personal success is indicated now, or else other people can't praise you highly enough. However, for different reasons you probably envisage a confrontation, especially if you have decided to take matters into your own hands. Whether you manage to get your own way or not, you are sure to make quite an impact.

4 FRIDAY Today Mercury will be moving into Aquarius, the financial area to your chart. Therefore, you could gain on matters related to travel, paperwork or the law, as will those born under the sign of Gemini or Virgo. Keep alert for the possibilities that the stars have in store for you. You won't regret it, I can assure you.

5 SATURDAY In some ways, what is implied between now the next couple of days is certain to hit home. You don't really know what you have done wrong, and you can be a bit touchy. Surely you are not that naive. If another person feels that you have been horrible to them, it would be nice if you extended the hand of friendship and love right now. Come on, pocket that pride.

6 SUNDAY Despite your best efforts to control certain situations, ultimately you must allow people to act or think for themselves. If you are approaching matters related to travel, you may not be able to observe what is going on in certain quarters. One thing is clear, it is bound to affect your immediate circumstances and those affected by them.

7 MONDAY Today Venus is lining up with Jupiter. These two are known as the 'greedy pigs of the zodiac', this means you could go well over the top with finances, with food, with booze and even with sex. Try to develop a sense of proportion and you can enjoy this day, if not you may find yourself a little bit ill.

8 TUESDAY There seems to have been a change of plan and you can't understand the logic going on behind it. You have talked about things thoroughly and now you don't know what to do. Certainly you will receive a clear message from the stars, and what's more you could be offered a much better option, one that is less trouble or easier to organize.

9 WEDNESDAY By rights you should be adequately compensated or be doing much better than you expected. That said, it will probably be what is suggested a little bit later that is of the most value to you, even if it means giving up something you would prefer to keep to yourself. You have every incentive to do so, so think about it.

10 THURSDAY The recent activity of the planets seems to be triggering some irrational responses from you, as well as from other people. You must be wondering exactly what you were thinking of, and how you're going to get yourself out of the situation. Follow your instincts and your imagination and act accordingly, even though some other people could take it as a bit of a joke – don't listen to them.

11 FRIDAY What is rumoured now sounds a bit insane, so wait until you've spoken to someone in person, as you may have been misinformed. Nevertheless, there will be some further rumblings during the next day or so, which again you are inclined to dismiss. This is understandable, but at least try to be as open-minded as you possibly can.

12 SATURDAY A dream, or vision, today should be taken seriously as it can guide you closer to your personal goals and ambitions. You'll find fulfilment in an unusual direction, so it's worth following wherever life takes you. By the end of next week you'll know exactly how to express your love in a way that's both romantic and meaningful. The other person will return the compliment with a practical gesture – it's still love, only in a different form. Sounds interesting!

13 SUNDAY Today is the day of the new Moon, and it occurs in your own sign of Capricorn. This should make this a really excellent day, and you will be ready to take on anyone and anything. It's also a good time to make a fresh start on important matters, as you are at your most charming and per-suasive right now.

14 MONDAY It may be January and traditionally a slow month of the year, but you're firing on all cylinders. If you're not fully into the swing of a lively social scene, there's some-thing wrong. Whether it's old friends or new, or all in the name of a good cause, you won't be staying in very much. When it comes to love, there's someone sweet and gentle waiting on the sidelines. It's a shame you're more interested in lust rather than romance.

15 TUESDAY It's an outstandingly brilliant day for your work and vocation, and you must take advantage of the opportunities coming your way. You may not get as good as this again for some time. Act fast, take some risks and you'll be on your way to the top. You may realize that you and someone special have different agendas now. You want a best friend, they want passion.

16 WEDNESDAY This is nothing less than a splendid day when everything you touch will turn to gold. Be original and inventive and you'll come out on top. In fact, if you're involved in a competition, you'll be a guaranteed winner; and in a work proposal you're the person for the job. Your star is in the ascendancy and it's time for you to show that success comes about through being unconventional and ahead of your time.

17 THURSDAY There are times when you're a lucky devil, and this is one of them. An opportunity will come your way today that you cannot turn down. It will mean having to get creative at work, but do it. It's just too good an opportunity to miss. In love, you're wise to finally break free from the past and give up your bad habits. Show someone special that you've turned over a new leaf.

18 FRIDAY Today Mercury goes into retrograde movement. You'd be most ill advised to take unnecessary trips or sign important paperwork for the time being, wait until this planet sees sense otherwise you'll be regretting it for several months to come, and that would be a great pity. If there's a Gemini or a Virgo in your life, they could be creating merry hell.

19 SATURDAY If a love affair is not working out, why give someone a second chance? Things will only go from bad to worse if you insist on hanging on in there. The stars suggest you're wise to move on and learn from your mistakes. But you're nothing if not a tenacious character, and you do tend to give people the benefit of the doubt. Just don't invest too much emotionally or financially at this time.

♑

20 SUNDAY That crazy game called love will continue to delight, amaze and shock you. Be prepared for anything, then nothing will come as too much of a surprise. You may be on the verge of falling head over heels in love, but you may be smitten by someone who can only be termed unconventional, or a partner may want to find a way to travel or pursue a spiritual path – anything goes. The game is just beginning.

21 MONDAY This could be an extremely good day for you, although it may not be money that's your good fortune. Instead, there'll be news of a baby, or a chance to show off your talents and be in the spotlight. You'll receive a gift as well, and its sentimental value will mean much more to you than any amount of money. Now is the time to remind yourself of all the good things that life brings – and to remember that it's the little things that mean so much.

22 TUESDAY An on-going battle with someone in your family will flare up today, and perhaps again later on. If someone's doing their best to split you and your partner up, they won't get far. Your bond is too strong, and you'll be proving it. Fond memories of the past will take you back to an idyllic haven. That time can come again, but it needs everyone's co-operation for harmony to reign.

23 WEDNESDAY Secrets and lies dominate during this day, and you'll need to question your part in the games that are taking place. Harmless fun is one thing, but cruelty for the sake of it is another. For a start, someone should stop a secret infatuation before it goes too far, although that's easier said than done. There is an important turning-point for a relationship very soon, but by then it will be too late to undo what is already done.

24 THURSDAY You prefer to consider all options before acting, but today this may not be possible. You could lose out financially if you're not prepared to take a risk and sign on the dotted line sooner rather than later. Don't put off until tomorrow what can be done today. But money means nothing where love is concerned. In fact, words mean everything and there's immense value in those three little words, 'I love you'.

25 FRIDAY This is a day when you will have the urge for a meaningful relationship. At work you'll thrive on creative moves and the ability to reinvent yourself again and again. Whatever passion you find on this particular day, you can be quite sure it's going to be a profound relationship with soul-searching and magical moments.

26 SATURDAY This is a time when you could be counting the cost of recent extravagances. However, it is unlikely that you will find yourself regretting any of them, because you don't believe in regrets now, do you? This evening brings new faces into your social life, which may prove particularly lucky for you if you find yourself involved in any type of team work. When it comes to romance, things look well starred, so make sure you keep a high profile.

27 SUNDAY The emphasis is on co-operation, especially with those people you might normally find difficult. Any failure to do so may make them even more obstinate than usual, so take it slowly and make it easy on yourself. This evening you will find your attention turning towards financial matters – about time, too.

28 MONDAY Today is the day of the full Moon. It occurs in the fiery sign of Leo, the area of your chart devoted to banking, finances which are shared and, to a degree, team effort. However, because the Moon is full there could be some obstacles in at least one of these areas, so do proceed warily.

29 TUESDAY This is a time when you will find you can make a fresh start and meet new faces. You'll be lurking near the limelight, but you need to make sure that this is for good reasons, not bad ones, so keep your ears close to the ground and don't worry about not being the centre of attention.

30 WEDNESDAY Someone you believe to be very close to emotionally, mentally or geographically, or even all three, is bottling up a great deal they need to release for their own peace of mind. You, too, may have a lot that you would like them to understand. Within a couple of days, though, there's going to be a sort of change or exchange. You might not be looking forward to it, but once this occurs you'll never look back on this time with anything but gratitude.

31 THURSDAY This seems to be an important day, when people are hanging on your every word and willing to do your every bidding. This evening will be a bit quiet; you may find yourself drumming your fingers and wondering what to do with yourself. But now is the time for rest, for encouraging your imagination and instincts, which you should listen to rather than your common sense.

FEBRUARY

Until 19 February the Sun will be drifting along in the airy sign of Aquarius, the area of your chart devoted to money. It won't be hard to chase that which is owed you, or to generate more cash if you so desire. Furthermore, should you find a small windfall, put it away in the bank for a rainy day.

From 19 January the Sun will be coasting along in Pisces, the area of your chart devoted to short journeys and the affairs of brothers and sisters. There'll be some new beginnings and changes taking place, so open up your mind, your heart and your arms and take it all on board. You'll be very glad that you did.

Mercury will be in retrograde movement until the 7th, therefore there's still a danger in paperwork, travel, or where people who were born under the sign of Gemini and Virgo are concerned. It's best that you mark time with your big ambitions and dreams until Mercury sees common sense.

Venus will be in Aquarius until 11 February, so during the early part of the month it's a good time for getting back money that's owed you and presenting ideas to other people. If you are asked to mix business with pleasure, do go ahead, otherwise you'll regret it.

On the 12th, Venus will move into Pisces, the area of your chart devoted to brothers and sisters and short journeys, all of which can be extremely lucky for you. Romance is casual, so don't start humming the Wedding March just yet, wait till things develop in the fullness of time.

Mars will be in Aries all month, the area of your chart devoted to home and property. There could be a certain amount of tension between yourself and relatives. Furthermore, if you're trying to negotiate moving house, or purchasing property, it's not going to be quite as straightforward as you'd thought. Then again, Capricorn, you are one of the most patient signs in the zodiac, so this shouldn't faze you too much.

The pattern made by the stars seems to be focusing on all your wishes, dreams, desires and schemes, so as long as you proceed one step at a time, as is your usual fashion, February can be a productive month. However, if you decide to speed things up then you could make mistakes and make a fool of yourself in front of other people. You really wouldn't like that one little bit now, would you?

1 FRIDAY There'll be some exciting news on this day, so you've got lots to look forward to – providing you stay alert, otherwise you'll miss out. You may also be taking part in some team event this evening which will prove to be very successful. It is also a great time for you to get out and make new friends. So if you're looking for Mr/Ms Right, now is the time to keep your eyes peeled.

2 SATURDAY The Moon suggests today that you will find yourself making a stand over a long drawn-out problem. You will also find yourself at your most ambitious at this time, and those around you could be in for something of a shock, while all along you smile secretly to yourself.

3 SUNDAY You seem to be in the limelight a little, but it's a good time for quiet contemplation, as very soon you will find yourself having to make some far-reaching decisions on the run, with not much time to consider the consequences. This evening you might be feeling a little under the weather, but providing you rest up and keep a sense of proportion there's no reason why you shouldn't bounce back very soon.

4 MONDAY Today Mercury will be moving into the earthy sign of Capricorn, the area of your chart devoted to the affairs of brothers and sisters and short journeys, all of which seem to be well starred. However, those of you who have fallen out with a relative recently may be wondering if you're ever going to make up. The answer is yes, but not just yet – you'll have to be patient.

5 TUESDAY The stars offer you a chance to re-think a plan and, when you do, you'll realize that you have overlooked something quite important. Just be thankful that you noticed before it was too late. This evening you'll be at your most adventurous, and because of this may find yourself making some rash promises to other people. At least you'll be making friends, but don't do so on the basis of any kind of deception.

6 WEDNESDAY The stars suggest today that you will be making a move with far-reaching consequences, or at least thinking about it, so make sure you think things through thoroughly. This evening is the time you may find yourself thinking about matters concerning friends or family abroad, or even booking a holiday in the near future. If you should be booking a trip, you'll get a bargain.

7 THURSDAY Today the stars offer you an opportunity to better yourself, so stay alert and grab whatever chances come your way or else you'll find yourself regretting it very soon. This evening your friends and colleagues are brimming with new ideas, so make sure you do plenty of listening and don't add your two penn'orth until you have all the facts and figures.

8 FRIDAY Luckily, today Mercury and Saturn decide to see sense and resume direct movement, so you need not fear short journeys, travel, booking a holiday or falling out with superiors from here on in. Life has been complicated enough lately, so don't imagine problems where none exist.

9 SATURDAY You may find yourself using intuition, instinct and your imagination; if you go along with these and the stars, you'll find yourself doing exceptionally well at this time. This evening sees an emphasis on team work and co-operation, so make sure that you consider other people's feelings before making any major decisions, otherwise you may find yourself in a bit of a difficult position later on.

10 SUNDAY If you are looking for action or excitement today, you'll find it, because the stars are now perfectly aligned. Whatever you decide to do on the spur of the moment may seem rather impulsive, but no doubt you have your reasons. Nonetheless, you may reach a point where someone won't allow you to go any further.

11 MONDAY By rights you should be elated by certain invitations or the advances of others. In truth, you never really expected someone to beg you to come back and try again. Not that you ever intended to. Besides, what takes place today means you will be inevitably drawn to one particular place where previously you had never dared venture.

12 TUESDAY Today is the day of the new Moon, and it occurs in your own sign. You'll be looking good, feeling good and ready to take on the world with one hand tied behind your back. Anything new that gets off the ground at this time,

♓

whether it's work or a new relationship, is extremely well starred, so push ahead and don't think twice.

13 WEDNESDAY You seem fairly happy to play along with everyone, even though this may mean having to fulfil certain commitments. Alternatively, you could just disappear and do your own thing. Partners or family members will expect you to make an effort this evening; it will be well worth it.

14 THURSDAY Today Mercury will be moving into Aquarius, the area of your chart devoted to money. You could be signing an important contract which will either take you abroad or perhaps give you a fresh start. If you want any advice, go to a Virgo or a Gemini; they have your best interests at heart, believe you me.

15 FRIDAY Seldom have you been so happy to be at home – it's just nice to be around the family, especially this evening. That said, there is one thing that could keep you away, though obviously you're not about to reveal what that is until all the details are confirmed. You still don't expect anyone to oppose your plans, even though this is a big step forward you're taking.

16 SATURDAY Admittedly there are still certain obstacles you need to overcome. Not that you go about it, as you suspect that others have not yet made a decision. Try to keep the lines of communication open. This evening there's every reason to believe that your entire situation is about to change for the better.

17 SUNDAY Perhaps there's only one option available to you now. Even though, in some respects, you admit it to be foolish to consider this, your anxiety could make you attempt anything. It's strange, but what happens over the next couple of days will be both difficult and divine.

18 MONDAY At first glance you are much more complicated than anyone thinks – and certainly you've been far more quiet and sedate than normal just recently. Because of the link between the planets, seldom will you have seemed so vibrant and others will openly encourage you to let go of the past.

19 TUESDAY Invitations for fun or romance seem to be coming in thick and fast, not only for today but also for the future. Those of you signing contracts connected with anything creative have done the right thing. This evening, romance is a distinct possibility, but there's an unreal feel about it. Don't get too carried away.

20 WEDNESDAY Something will happen today which will give you plenty of food for thought. You will realize that the reason for living is to do something positive. Do your best to prove that the world would be a sadder place without you. Remember that you are original, there is only one you, and that you are here to fill a certain need, either in the life of someone else or by contributing to the world in general.

21 THURSDAY Your attempts to uncover detailed information about a specific situation might not amount to very much. You're probably more than content to remain in the background at this moment in time and let somebody else steer the action. Nevertheless, it would be a good idea this evening to get out and let off some steam.

22 FRIDAY As you're finding out, probably to your embarrassment, certain facts and figures simply don't add up. It's possible, of course, that this may not be a case of deliberate distortion or corruption, but even the simplest mistake right now can cost you dearly and mustn't be permitted to happen again under any circumstances.

23 SATURDAY Work seems to be routine, therefore you'll have plenty of energy for enjoyment tonight. If nothing is planned, why not invite a few friends around? You need stimulating conversation and perhaps the opportunity to pick somebody else's brains too. Romance is reasonably well starred, but don't allow your expectations to take flight.

24 SUNDAY This is likely to be a day of heightened sensitivity and awareness, which could leave you feeling unappreciated. Plans to change your lifestyle are likely to be frowned upon by those closest to you, but at least you know what you want and need. All you have to do now is to convince them that you know what you're talking about, because you most certainly do.

25 MONDAY As a Capricorn, you should always use your intuition though you are invariably reluctant to do so. Right now, a powerful hunch has probably led you to spot ways to capitalize on your talents. Unfortunately, events are moving so quickly you may have missed the boat. Keep an eye on developments and be ready to move at the first sign of activity. Next time you must be the first one off the mark.

26 TUESDAY Today you need to accept the fact that feelings of aggression and injustice have flared up, not because of you but in spite of you. Never mind, your morale should be improving soon. Make every effort to keep things moving, no matter what opposition you may meet. If nothing occurs, at least it will not be for the want of trying.

27 WEDNESDAY There's one thing about you, Capricorn, which the rest of us cannot deny: you are the most loyal and faithful of friends. However, separation seems to have been a lot in your life recently, but rest assured that surprise developments are about to reverse this unfortunate trend and restore, or at least repair, relationships which have been pulled about through carelessness or misunderstanding.

28 THURSDAY For one reason or another you really can't take advantage of the fact that you're at your most ambitious except, possibly, by inviting colleagues around for a drink or even a meal. This evening is a good time for making plans for the near and distant future. Other people will be putting in their two penn'orth, but in a constructive way.

MARCH

Until 20 March the Sun will be drifting along in the water sign of Pisces, the area of your chart connected with the affairs of brothers and sisters, short journeys, trips and casual romance. Any, or all, of these are likely to be lucky for you, but not particularly long-lived, so bear that in mind.

After 20 March the Sun will be sizzling along in the fiery sign of Aries, the area of your chart devoted to home, family and property affairs. Some of you may be thinking of moving from one area to another, while others are getting ready to entertain friends on the home front, and doing so with a certain amount of style which people will not forget.

Mercury is in a restless mood, and is in Aquarius for the first 11 days of the month. This, of course, is the money area of your chart, so if you're signing any important documents or going to a meeting you should be fairly lucky.

From 12 to 29 March, Mercury will be making its way into Pisces. You'll find it extremely difficult to sit still. Paperwork and travel will be extremely important to your career, and people you meet while going from place to place could become firm friends in a short space of time. Those of you who are unattached will be meeting new people who have some novel ideas; a lot of fun seems to be in store.

Venus is in Pisces until the 7th, once more emphasizing the area of life devoted to communications and short trips. On a romantic level, you'll be bumping into some very attractive people, so much so that you really won't be able to make up your mind as to which relationship you want to develop. There's no need to rush, Capricorn. Take things a step at a time, as you usually do, and you'll make the right decision. Then these relationships could be made to last a little longer than just a night.

On 8 March Venus moves on into the fiery sign of Aries, where it will stay until the end of the month. This is the time when you might want to do some redecorating or home improvements. Alternatively, why not just invite some friends round to enjoy your home with you? If you have children who have been more demanding than usual of late, now is the time to make them see reason.

Mars will be in the earth sign of Taurus from 2 March, the area of your chart devoted to matters related to children, creativity, sport, fun and games in general and casual romance. Mind you, those hormones are whizzing through your veins at an alarming rate, so don't plan on falling in love – well, not for some while anyway. Allow new relationships to stand the test of time before you give your tender heart away. You may look very big and tough on the outside, but that is a complete lie, inside you can be as wobbly as jelly when it comes to the personal side to life.

The pattern made by the stars seems to be concentrating on your personal life rather than ambitions, so give them a rest for the time being. You'll achieve a great deal later on; for now you can rest on your laurels. In the mean time you can make plans for the future, but don't act for the time being, wait until the stars are more on your side. You're one sign that hates to fail – let's face it, for you ambition is a personal thing, not an objective one.

1 FRIDAY Because you have learned to take the rough with the smooth, you are unlikely to be left high and dry, or to lose your sense of direction. Your vision, plus your vivid imagination, are your greatest gifts at the moment. You must not forget that what you can imagine right now can be accomplished in the very near future.

2 SATURDAY Today Mars will be moving into Taurus, where it will stay for the rest of the month, in the area of your chart devoted to matters related to children, sport, casual romance and artistic endeavours. However, don't be in too much of a rush. If you are, you could make some horrible mistakes and will be kicking yourself for quite some time, not to mention looking a little foolish in the eyes of others.

ƥ

3 SUNDAY Today's stars make it obvious that others are perfectly happy for you to take control and put all your vitality into improving what appears to be an unrealistic and difficult situation. What's more, your efforts can't fail to be rewarded in some way in the future.

4 MONDAY Today those grey cells of yours will be hopping about like demented Mexican jumping beans. You need plenty to keep you busy, otherwise you'll become bored and a bit tetchy. This is a great time for travelling or taking on a fresh challenge or course of learning. New people you meet during the day and evening will be fascinating, as well as handing on some useful tips. Romance is casual, so don't take it too seriously. What seems to be a mundane period is likely to prove to be exactly the opposite.

5 TUESDAY You continue to be full of brilliant ideas, and this will help you no end in dealing quickly with paperwork and decisions that have been tossed to one side for some considerable while now. Believe me, Capricorn, you really are on the ball now, and this is of great benefit when it comes to understanding those who are considerably younger than yourself, or perhaps simply less experienced. Yes, you will be providing the guiding light for someone else who, in the near future, is likely to be forever grateful.

6 WEDNESDAY Some of you may get the chance to do some business travelling. If not, it's a great time for meeting colleagues in order to thrash out differences in a civilized fashion. Even professional contacts will be useful and, although there's a distinct possibility that you won't see the

positive results for your efforts, at least this evening you can
make friends again with someone who has been oddly remote
recently.

7 THURSDAY The stars may be undermining your enthusiasm and your energy. The best thing to do is to take life at an
easy pace and relax. After all, what's the point of tearing
around after other people, especially if they don't seem to be
making any effort to contact you? Those Capricorns taking
part in sport need to be particularly careful, as bad judgement
could lead to minor injuries.

8 FRIDAY You get the green light from the stars to step into
the spotlight. Luckily, those closest to you, both at work and
at home, seem to be in a positive and sunny frame of mind;
this makes them very approachable, so if you need to ask for
favours or even make romantic overtures, then this is the time
to do so. This evening the phone is likely to be red hot, and
it's difficult to imagine you opting to stay at home quietly
behaving yourself.

9 SATURDAY It's the Capricorn who'll be working according
to long-made, carefully thought out plans who will be doing
best at this time. Unusually, you are able to separate your
emotions from your ambitions; this can be no bad thing and,
because of it, your progress could be nothing short of spec-
tacular. This evening the words of an older person will give
you food for thought.

10 SUNDAY Cash matters should be a good deal less complicated, as well as less disappointing. Mind you, it may take
you a while to sort out the current mess, but you've enough

determination and savvy, as well as patience, to do so. If you're waiting for the right time to make an important move, professionally or personally, then it has finally arrived. Don't hesitate to leap into action.

11 MONDAY You're feeling very physical at the moment, both sexy and aggressive, so heaven help anybody who tries to stall your progress over the next few days or so. The stars bode well for manual or for sporty types because energy levels rise quite dramatically. There's a possibility, too, that your hormones will be stirred on the slightest pretext. You need to exercise a certain amount of control, or at least recognize the fact that this is the old devil 'sex' in action rather than any finer emotions.

12 TUESDAY Today Mercury will be moving into the watery sign of Pisces, the area of your chart devoted to brothers, sisters, short journeys and good ideas. You'll find it extremely difficult to sit still at this time, but why bother, because while keeping on the go you'll fall into opportunities and meet interesting people.

13 WEDNESDAY Those closest to you will be at their most sensitive, intuitive and sentimental. Soften your approach to them, be more considerate and, if you do have someone special waiting for you, give them plenty of attention and your evening will be one to remember for quite some while. If you are single, keep a high profile because it won't be difficult to find someone who sets your heart racing.

14 THURSDAY Today is the day of the new Moon, and it occurs in the water sign of Pisces, the area of your chart

devoted to matters related to brothers and sisters, short journeys and inspiration. These aspects of life seem to be very
important this month, so don't neglect them at all, and
remember with new Moons it's always a great time for
making fresh starts.

15 FRIDAY This could very well turn out to be a red letter
day. You have more confidence, know-how and ability than
anyone else you come into contact with right now. Be brave
then, Capricorn, and don't hesitate to present your ideas to all
and sundry, because others will be amazed at your ingenuity
and will be anxious to be part of your schemes. You can
expect to be courted quite seriously by others, although
you're not fool enough to be taken in by false flattery or silver
tongues.

16 SATURDAY Over the next couple of days you must think
twice about travel plans, legal matters and paperwork in general, because these are all areas which could prove to be sources
of irritation, aggravation and maybe even loss. If you can procrastinate where such matters are concerned, so much the
better; be prepared to mark time. Even if you begin to tear your
hair out with frustration, it's still the wisest course to take.

17 SUNDAY A phase in life could be coming to an end, or
perhaps somebody has decided to move on. This is certainly
not a time for looking for a new home because you could
make a gigantic mistake. Try to be content with life as it is for
the time being because, after all, the stars change very quickly
so being patient for a while isn't too much to ask.

18 MONDAY Today it's the softer and more courteous approach to other people that will pay off. You'll be able to brush aside differences with colleagues, relatives and even loved ones, and there's a definite coming together between yourself and other people. Clearly then, if you're fancy-free you must get out and about this evening, because it's a great time for romance and you would hate to miss out, wouldn't you?

19 TUESDAY Today you may find other people being anything but straightforward and honest with you. You may find several new admirers, but each and every one of them may have somebody else tucked away in the background – and you know how much you love deception. It's something you simply can't cope with, because you're a straightforward, loyal and honest person yourself and you can't see any reason why others should be different.

20 WEDNESDAY You can certainly expect a hectic or even frantic time on the work front, although you will find the increased level of activity stimulating. There's no doubt there'll be plenty of discussion going on which should benefit you in the end. This evening you will want to share as much as possible with the special person in your life, and they certainly seem to be in a receptive mood, so a cozy evening is predicted. On the other hand, if you're unattached this is no time for sitting at home brooding. Let yourself get caught up in the social whirl.

21 THURSDAY Today the Sun will be moving into the fiery sign of Aries and the area of your chart devoted to home, property, family and (to a degree) the mind. This is an excellent period for entertaining friends or colleagues at home, and you'll be doing yourself a great deal of good, so at least think about doing so.

22 FRIDAY You've got a couple of good days if you are a free-lance worker, or the Capricorn who is looking for work, so step up your efforts because you could be successful. There's a possibility, too, of finding a new ambition or objective in life, one that fills you with enthusiasm, vitality and hope for the future. Friends will be very supportive, so if you need favours from them, this is the time to ask.

23 SATURDAY If you're spending time at home, the atmosphere could be tense and electric. It looks as if unspoken words are making everyone unhappy, so why don't you sit down with the person concerned and talk through disagreements or differences of opinion? When all is said and done, it's the grown-up thing to do. If you ignore this advice you'll find yourself overwrought by the time bedtime arrives.

24 SUNDAY Where work is concerned, don't be over-confident. It might also be a good idea to double-check complicated tasks, because mistakes can be made. This evening the arrogant side of your character may surface, and this proves to be off-putting, not only to loved ones but also to potential admirers.

25 MONDAY The stars are likely to be filling you with confidence, hope and positive thoughts. This is an especially lucky time to take decisions on behalf of loved ones, and it's good, too, for attending interviews, negotiations and meetings. Don't be afraid to make bold moves with a certain style, because this will appeal to other people at this time and make them want to be involved in all your ambitious plans. Nice to be so popular.

26 TUESDAY Do be sure that you are scrupulous and answer all phone calls and messages. Read your mail thoroughly too. Those of you provided with a chance for travel, don't hesitate to say 'yes' in a loud voice. New people you meet at this time will be important to your destiny as well as your personal life. Mix with the human race a little more frequently than you usually do, because you most certainly won't be sorry if you do.

27 WEDNESDAY Your imagination takes flight and you'll be thinking up original ways of generating more money. These will pay off in the not too distant future. New people you meet during this day will be important to you, as will paperwork. Somebody close to you is over-confident this evening and you may have to apply a restraining, but gentle hand, before they become too carried away and make a major decision which could be unfortunate.

28 THURSDAY This is the day of the full Moon and it occurs in the airy sign of Libra, the area of your chart devoted to work and prestige. Double-check everything, because if you make a mistake you'll be made to look a fool in front of your colleagues, and that simply won't do for a proud Capricorn, I think you'll admit. It's also a good time for putting the finishing touches to work that has been hanging around for a long time.

29 FRIDAY No matter where you go today, you're going to be meeting up with confident, optimistic and smiling faces. Even if your own mood is a little gloomy, this is only a temporary state of affairs because it won't take long before the mood of those around you proves to be infectious and brightens you up no end. Because of this, it would be a good idea to make certain that you're out and about this evening, because the more you circulate the easier it will be for you to let off steam and have some fun.

30 SATURDAY You know, Capricorn, you could be quite irresistible today; all you've got to do is to believe it. This is a good time for presenting your ideas to loved ones and also planning for changes in the future. Paperwork that has been ignored to date can be signed with confidence, and this evening is certainly a great time for romance. Keep in circulation.

31 SUNDAY What seems to be a harmless remark may not be so innocent after all. Be distrustful of rumours which are making the rounds too and, perhaps above all else, you need to pay attention to details, particularly if you're planning something special. With the right approach you can be positively inspired in your thinking today, and will experience success on a personal level.

APRIL

Until 19 April the Sun will be drifting along in the fiery sign of Aries, in the area of your chart devoted to home, property and family matters. Furthermore, you'll be inclined to entertain on your home base rather than travelling too far away. Perhaps you're trying to conserve energy, time and money. That's not a bad idea, as long as you don't get too miserly about it.

From 20 April the Sun will be drifting along in Taurus, the area of your chart devoted to children, creativity, casual

romance and sport. All, or some of these, may take prec-
edence during this period, but most of them should be
extremely lucky for you, so don't lose confidence.

Mercury will be in Aries until 12 April, in the area of your
chart devoted to home. There's a lot of movement and change
going on there. Maybe you're decorating, or perhaps inviting
friends around for a drink or a meal. Either way you seem to
be enjoying yourself, surely no bad thing.

On 13 April Mercury will move into the earthy sign of
Taurus, and will stay there for the rest of the month. This will
be a stimulating time for intellectual pursuits and pastimes, as
well as sporting activities. If there is a Taurus among your
family or friends, they will be most receptive to requests for
help right now.

Venus will be in Taurus until 25 April, in the area of your
life devoted to sport, matters related to children, and love
affairs. Some of you may even be thinking about making a
serious commitment, but don't do so under the influence of
alcohol; wait until you're seeing things clearly and, if you still
feel this is the right thing to do, then go for it.

On 26 April Venus moves on into Gemini. Oh, dear! You
do have a tendency to be a bit of a greedy pig; you really will
have to watch yourself just now. Your health should be all
right if you don't over-indulge – remember, it's easy to put
others off by your behaviour.

Mars is in Taurus until 13 April, so do take care if you're
taking part in sport; you could be bruised, cut, etc.
Furthermore, try not to be too strict with young children, you
were young yourself remember, and I don't suppose you were
any more organized or virtuous than your own brood are.
Furthermore, Mars could make you fall in lust, rather than in
love, and this is never satisfactory for you although you may

kid yourself it is. Still, providing you don't give your heart away too easily, there's no reason why you shouldn't enjoy yourself, so see that you do.

From the 14th Mars joins Venus in the airy sign of Gemini. This is a rather tiring influence and you may feel at a low ebb. It would be as well to keep a low profile and stay away from anyone who is ill or who is in a grumpy mood.

The pattern made by the stars places the emphasis on Aries and Taurus this month. If you have these signs in your life, they are likely to be playing an important role during this particular period. Well, you can't always have the limelight, though luckily you don't always expect it, so play the supporting role and try to look interested even though what others are talking about are way beyond you. You'll gain a great deal in the way of love, respect and gratitude.

1 MONDAY Today you're going to be more prepared to listen to the advice and words of contacts rather than insisting on going on your own sweet way regardless of what other people think. There's a possibility that this evening you will meet new people who will affect your life in a major way in the near future. If you're single, you couldn't have a better time for visiting a club, because this could lead to romance. Not that it's likely to be the 'love of your life', but it'll do for the time being – simply enjoy yourself.

2 TUESDAY Meeting emotional duties is giving you a few headaches. It's not that you can't live up to the expectations of other people, but you don't want to cause a scene simply because you feel you're under siege. You have more than enough staying power and, besides, others will soon back down, then you can lower the drawbridge and get on with living.

3 WEDNESDAY If someone is playing hard to get or simply being awkward, then it's not your fault. Be prepared to boost their confidence a little and they could turn their face towards you, rather than away. They're wrapped in possibilities and dreams, while you're trying to be realistic. Of course the present matters, but so does a person's vision of tomorrow.

4 THURSDAY Although you suspect that your working life must change, there seems little you can do about it. Knuckling down to run-of-the-mill matters will help you focus on the future. The planets are only too aware of how impulsive you can be at times, but with a practical approach and some admiration from others, you're on the road to bigger things.

5 FRIDAY Show someone special that you're not on automatic pilot, but are as autonomous and free-thinking as they are. If others don't realize why you need to be free to enjoy certain romantic notions, then they have only themselves to blame. You are in an excellent position to establish how liberated you can be when you choose.

6 SATURDAY There are aspects of your private life which demand your attention. Taking the easy way out won't come easily. After all, you prefer to be more radical about certain issues. Keeping an open mind is probably the best line. It's hardly likely to cause too much of a dispute, and that's better than wounded feelings.

7 SUNDAY It seems like a foolproof transaction could become a bone of contention. It seems more realistic to take a dynamic approach rather than maintaining a passive attitude. Results are forthcoming, but only if you stop others from dominating the floor. You need to boost your spirits and show you actually mean business now.

8 MONDAY The next couple of days could produce all the signs and signals you need to realize why one intimate relationship is improving. It's not that you're unduly worried, but are aware there are certain issues that need resolving. Trust in your open approach to life. Your optimistic side is about to be given a boost. And with that comes a better understanding of why others admire your qualities. You feel so much better with this knowledge.

9 TUESDAY Others are beginning to respect your sometimes risqué attitude towards finances. Especially as you're in a situation which requires you either to leap forward and initiate a new venture, or to stay as you are. It won't come as a surprise to others to find out exactly which you'd rather do. Whatever you choose, you'll get a few people talking.

10 WEDNESDAY It's fine if others need your support and organizational talent, but the last thing you want now is to become a dog's body. Anyone who is becoming despotic won't win your approval. But the planets are urging you to stick to your own methods. It would be appropriate to inform others that you're not ready to back down now – and probably never will.

11 THURSDAY Light and breezy though you may be on the surface, underneath you are less tolerant of someone's assumptions about you. It would, of course, be easier to retreat and let them think they've scored a few points. But resentment will only build up if you don't sort it out. Try to make it a rational discussion rather than an all-out wrangle. You won't regret it.

12 FRIDAY Today is the day of the new Moon and it occurs in the fiery sign of Aries, the area of your chart devoted to home. There are likely to be some positive changes going on there. If you're in the throes of negotiating property affairs, you've picked an ideal time for pushing ahead. It's always good to make fresh starts when there is a new Moon, and this one is no exception.

13 SATURDAY Pitting yourself against a complex suggestion could be more demanding than you imagine. Becoming unnerved because others think they know best won't resolve anything. If you believe that it's easier to give way and be generous, then fine. But this is a time when it would be wise to probe your own motives for doing so first, then you won't be disappointed.

14 SUNDAY There's little point expecting certain people to understand your desire to be challenged. You have a flair for being stretched to the limit, and you're not going to give up now. You're better off staying independent – the rewards will be greater.

15 MONDAY Perseverance is called for, now you're facing another undertaking. More than likely you'll succeed, just trust your feelings on this one. In fact, you now have the ability to convince others of your real mission. And that means being true to your beliefs and maintaining your equilibrium. It will be worth the effort.

16 TUESDAY You're on automatic pilot today because your mind is on other things – namely love and romance. Whether you're planning a special night with your other half, or looking forward to seeing someone you fancy, the good news is that luck is on your side. The evening will be an important one for your future, and you may even look back on it as a turning-point in your life.

17 WEDNESDAY Today you can't afford to be over-confident about your own ability or judgement. If you're self-employed, or on a bonus scheme, don't miss out on an opportunity to make some extra money. It will be up to you to take full advantage of a lucky break. This evening, focus on being sociable and enjoying yourself. If you're in a relationship, a night out with pals will be great fun. If you're looking to meet someone new, tonight could be the night.

18 THURSDAY Your ability to turn your hand to almost anything is going to put you in the boss' good books today, as well, perhaps, as those of loved ones. If you can take on extra work and make it look easy, you'll earn some brownie points and improve your chances of a pay rise. There's a great evening in store, especially if you are out with friends. This looks like being a red letter day for your love life, especially if you're single.

19 FRIDAY Listen out for news of changes starting to happen at work, especially at the top. A new boss will prove to be a proverbial new broom, keen to sweep clean from the word go. The good news is that these changes will be for the better as far as you're concerned. Your job satisfaction will zoom if you hang on in there. This evening it is party time, which gives you a chance to meet an interesting selection of new people.

20 SATURDAY Even if you don't have much to show for it in terms of solid results, you should still feel it's been a productive day. The irons you put in the fire are red hot, and some of your ideas are positively inspired – even if you haven't quite realized it yet. Don't be too impatient, because everything will work out well. Your love life is also promising, especially if you're making a conscious effort to be there for your partner.

21 SUNDAY The Sun is now in the earthy sign of Taurus, the area of your chart devoted to creativity, matters related to children, good times and casual romance. From hereon in, don't take others' promises too seriously, simply be light-hearted and kick up your heels for a change.

22 MONDAY Recent events have been telling you that you need to take a whole lot more control of your love life. Whether you want a better sex life or you're looking for a new relationship, it's all about recognizing which choices you're facing. For some of you, this will mean either sticking with what you've got or making a break. Either way, a fresh start is needed. You need to let your partner know how serious you are. A lot hinges on what kind of response you get. And if a lover has already had a second chance, how many excuses can you make for them?

℔

23 TUESDAY You get an invitation which you simply can't refuse. Mind you, when you finally manage to dredge up the energy to join in, you'll be very glad you did. This is especially so if you're unattached, because your chances of meeting someone you're attracted to are high. You could very well end the night in a state of great excitement, knowing that this is the start of something big.

24 WEDNESDAY It seems you've had the upper hand in your love life for quite a while – and you've done a good job of getting your relationships in shape. But don't under-estimate the importance of letting your partner know when they've done something that makes you happy. The first big pay-off of feeling closer is great sex, and you may decide to spend this evening in bed rather than in the bar. If you're unattached, there are plenty of special flings in the offing which could easily turn into something more important.

25 THURSDAY Misunderstandings of any kind can be cleared up quickly today; your ability to speak the unvarnished truth will stand you in good stead. Loved ones always value your opinion or advice more than you realize, if only because they know you always say what you think.

26 FRIDAY If you're single, this evening the stars will bring you a golden opportunity to go out on the prowl. Find out where the party is – or create one of your own. You may get carried away and overdo it, which will leave you wiped out for the rest of the week, but what a nice way to go!

27 SATURDAY Today is the day of the full Moon, and it occurs in the water sign of Scorpio, the area of your chart

℔

devoted to friends and team effort, though it might be difficult to get things off the ground. It wouldn't be a good idea to take part in team sports during this particular day, as there could be some minor accidents and you don't want to finish up 'poorly'.

28 SUNDAY You'll have your serious hat on at work today; there's plenty to do and you will certainly be earning every penny. But once the whistle blows, you'll be out that door as fast as lightning – and all geared up for a great evening. Whether this is something you've had planned in advance, or a spontaneous get-together, you're in for a great time. You could even be tempted to fit in two events tonight. You're spoiled for choice – and why not?

29 MONDAY Your opinion is being sought at work, although this doesn't mean it will count for very much at the end of the day. Still, it's important to have your say and, if necessary, to go on record about what you think should be done over the next couple of days. You may find you need to refer back to the events or a decision you've made recently. Home is where the heart is for you this evening, whether you want to cuddle up with your other half or invite friends over.

30 TUESDAY Whatever you do today, don't play second fiddle to a bossy lover or colleague. You have your own ambitions and you must make them top priority. Today you'll start to sow the seeds of future prosperity and must protect what is yours. Soon you'll be able to develop the loving side of your character more fully.

MAY

This month the Sun will be scooting along in the earthy sign of Taurus until the 20th, the area of your chart devoted to matters related to children, creativity, sport and good times in general. Mind you, you shouldn't take new faces too seriously, they're ridiculously flirty and you could get hurt if you jump in head-first, so be a little bit cautious and all should go well.

From 21 May the Sun will be moving along into the airy sign of Gemini, the area of your chart devoted to health matters and sheer hard slog. Of course, you are a hard worker and that's to be applauded. If you sense that your body is beginning to run down, for heaven's sake be kind to it, otherwise you'll regret it at a later date.

Mercury will be in Gemini all month. You'd be very ill-advised to start signing any kind of important documents or undertaking any unnecessary travel after the 15th, because at that time Mercury goes into retrograde movement and you know how difficult that can be for you. Be as patient as you can, you've plenty of the right stuff when you really try.

Venus will be in Gemini up until 20 May, in the area of your chart devoted to work. If you're in a professional partnership or your job is at all artistic, you'll be doing well. Grab all the opportunities to socialize with work contacts, as you'll be doing yourself a bit of good.

From 21 May onwards, Venus will be moving into Cancer, throwing a rosy glow over all relationships. Some of you may even be prepared to 'name the day', but don't do so in a rush because, if you do, you'll be heading for the divorce courts further down the line – and you really don't want that now, do you?

Until 27 May, Mars will be in Gemini. Look after yourself, particularly when you're in the kitchen. Make sure that you don't overwork because if you do, your body will give out at some point and you'll be missing out on all of the fun that you were looking forward to, which would be a great pity. Certainly, if you are a sportsperson strains and sprains could be the norm, and that may be inconvenient. You'll have to mollycoddle yourself until you're better, otherwise you will be making a big mistake.

1 WEDNESDAY Certainly where matters associated with your children are concerned, socializing and romance could become unduly complicated. But never mind, Capricorn, there are moments when you enjoy a challenge and this is one of them, so get the bit between your teeth, dredge up your tenacity and nothing will be able to stall your progress. It could be a good idea to double-check all long-standing arrangements, just in case.

2 THURSDAY If other people seem to think of you as something of a plodder, that's because you are cautious and you like to think things through from every possible angle. But, let's face it, you can be as imaginative as the next person, as you are about to prove today, perhaps to somebody else's surprise. This evening looks promising for romance, so if you are unattached do make certain that you are out there in the big wide world circulating, otherwise you could seriously miss out and that would never do.

3 FRIDAY You've a wonderful day for asking favours from contacts and friends and even workmates. Because of your stars today there might be a tendency to keep yourself to yourself, but you will need somebody else at times, so leap out of your shell and mix with the human race – you'll find a warm welcome waiting for you, I can assure you.

4 SATURDAY Maybe you've got something special to look forward to this evening and that is why there's a spring in your step and a gleam in your eye. It's a good time, too, for matters related to children or creative work, and these should go without a hitch. Make this day count; you'll be glad that you did.

5 SUNDAY It might be a good idea for you to remember that you could be focusing too intensely on professional matters and, unusually, neglecting loved ones. If you succumb to this common pitfall, you could find a full rebellion on your hands on and off throughout this time. Best to balance your life equally between work, play and family; if you do, you'll achieve a great deal.

6 MONDAY Today you'd be wise to let events take their own course rather than trying to influence them in any way. Your mood is never particularly good with certain influences, and it is important that you control your active imagination. See what you can do.

7 TUESDAY If you're a parent or teacher, you should find it relatively easy to sort out a muddle or some confusion in connection with a child. As for other Capricorns, be certain you're looking your best at all times, because romance seems to be knocking at your door and you'd hate to be caught off-guard, as you tend to be a self-conscious individual. Play your astrological cards right and this could be a very good day.

8 WEDNESDAY Discipline and self-restraint are necessary now in order to avoid wasting money and possessions. Where partnerships certainly look promising for long-term success, it's best to leave contractual matters for the time being. At work, irritations may cause rash behaviour and speech; this is due to your own emotional insecurities and it's up to you to recognize this fact, otherwise you may feel that others are being demanding. Discussion could very well ease the situation, so think about it.

9 THURSDAY The time is right for making minor changes where ambitions and work matters are concerned. If you're unemployed, for heaven's sake step up your efforts because meetings and negotiations can be extremely successful. All you need is that extra little bit of belief in yourself, so talk to someone, perhaps an admirer, because this will help to give you the edge and bring about success.

10 FRIDAY You may find yourself at odds with people you meet while going about your everyday duties, and colleagues are likely to be highly sensitive. Bite your sarcastic tongue and consider the feelings of other people, because this certainly isn't a time for being too blunt. Certainly it's a lively day, and an even more lively evening. Romance is a possibility if you're single, but please don't get too carried away.

11 SATURDAY Your interaction with groups of friends should be enjoyable and productive now. The only problem is, you must control a tendency to be over-critical even if you feel let down in some way. Perhaps it is your own fault, because your expectations were too high in the first place. It might be a good idea, too, to take some time to examine yourself and what you have learned from the influence from other people. I think you'll find it's a great deal.

12 SUNDAY Today is the day of the new Moon, and it occurs in the earthy sign of Taurus, the area of your chart devoted to children, creativity, sport and casual romance. Any, or all, of these may see new beginnings and, if so, it's going to be an extremely lively day and a happy one too.

13 MONDAY Compliments will be plentiful today. You act powerfully and effectively in the outside world, while at the same time keeping a quiet, watchful eye on the background. Social life and romance are certainly favoured this evening. You can attract friends effortlessly. Just beware that a particularly possessive attitude doesn't jeopardize these wonderful opportunities.

14 TUESDAY You certainly seem to be in good form today, so make strides to accomplish personal goals, those which are important to you. Relationships could feel a bit obsessive; remember that you are a separate person, and so are they. Impatience over delays and finishing projects will need controlling too. The root of a problem, and some considerable tension, is probably money.

15 WEDNESDAY Mercury is now in retrograde movement, so until it sees common sense for heaven's sake don't travel unnecessarily, sign paperwork or go on any kind of interview. If you do, you'll be playing your own worst enemy. Don't say I didn't warn you.

16 THURSDAY Situations and people will not be how they appear. Although it's true that somebody may be out to deceive you, in the main it's simply a case of most of your contacts being in an indecisive and wishy-washy frame of mind. There's no point in bullying them, or even trying to persuade them, they'll come out of this mood in their own good time and without any help from you, thank you very much.

17 FRIDAY Cash opportunities could help you to reorganize your life in a more constructive way. Your values are likely to go through a fundamental shift now. Think carefully about responsibilities as well as what you want and need. Over the next couple of days, family activity will demand much of your time and energy, but you'll feel more valued.

18 SATURDAY Don't be too proud to ask for someone's advice, because what you hear will certainly set you back on the right track. Many of you will be taking on a more serious attitude to a relationship, and some may even be ready to make a commitment. Any way you look at it, it's certainly going to be an interesting time.

19 SUNDAY This is a time when you can chase your own desires, wants and needs without feeling guilty. It will be a particularly productive time for those who are self-employed. All born under this sign should chase their dreams, because there's a possibility that you can make them come true.

20 MONDAY A good sense of timing and an enterprising spirit will help you to make progress and restore confidence. Expect recognition for imaginative ideas, which you communicate and apply well during the day. An artistic mood may very well be nourished by nature so, where possible, get out into the open and look at your environment with new eyes.

21 TUESDAY Today Venus will be moving into the water sign of Cancer, your opposite sign. There is a healthy, rosy glow over all relationships, be they romantic, professional or otherwise. This is an excellent time for asking for any kind of favour if necessary, so don't hesitate, push ahead.

22 WEDNESDAY The Sun has now moved into Gemini, the area of your chart devoted to work and health. If you've been feeling under the weather, you're certainly going to be picking up over the next few days or so. Furthermore, relationships with workmates are going to be on the up and up. Co-operation is always important, of course, so this is nice.

23 THURSDAY You're surrounded by enthusiastic faces and minds which are bursting with ideas. This may make you feel a little inadequate, but you can't always be on top form, Capricorn. Even you need a rest, and this is an ideal time for doing just that. Why don't you turn your attention to having fun? It is permitted, you know, and it always helps you to return to work feeling refreshed, replenished, renewed and with even greater ambition.

24 FRIDAY Look for the advantageous moves at work and in money, but avoid overwork because strains and stresses, or angry criticism, could affect your health. Keep on the move, enjoy socializing, romance or outdoor activities; these will all help to offset any negative influences and put you back on the road to recovery and positive thinking.

♑

25 SATURDAY The last thing you should do today is mix business with pleasure in any way, shape or form. Keep these two compartments of your life completely separate and know when to switch off ambition (on returning home this evening). Failure to do so will only irritate loved ones who have been waiting for you with open, loving arms; they don't want to be assailed with your success or failures of the day, well not just now anyway.

26 SUNDAY This is the day of the full Moon and it occurs in the fiery sign of Sagittarius, the area of your chart devoted to what is going on in the background of things. Root around and make sure that you are in the know, because not to be could make you look foolish in the eyes of your workmates and your boss, and we don't want that now, do we?

27 MONDAY What is happening in the background is what is important, although you may be unaware of this for the time being. Keep an eye open for signals that others are perhaps considering changing direction, or maybe even moving on, because this could affect your own prospects for the future. This evening it's likely you'll decide to rest up and replenish yourself, and you couldn't have a better time for doing that.

28 TUESDAY Remember today that life is too short to find yourself on one end of a tug-of-war when somewhere else there are people who understand your values and are not constantly trying to engage you in some kind of pointless competition. This is a day for refusing to take the bait.

29 WEDNESDAY The stars seem to augur well for future success. Any changes you want to make in any area of life should be implemented as soon as possible, because at this time, Capricorn, you really can't go wrong. A minor new cycle may be starting right now, though you may be unaware of the fact for at least a couple of days. You're at your most attractive, too, so if you want to make romantic moves, this is the time.

30 THURSDAY Today you have some extra magic and charisma about you that few can resist, and if you want a time for getting your own way, asking for favours or chasing somebody you have had your eye on for some time, this is it. Remember, he who hesitates is lost; make sure this doesn't happen to you at this moment in time.

31 FRIDAY Trying to steer a middle road is never easy for you. Your natural tendency is to throw yourself wholeheartedly into both relationships and work. But do remember, Capricorn, that you are a creature of extremes and, difficult though they may be to control, it would be a foolhardy Goat who didn't take a good careful look before leaping ahead into life at this time.

JUNE

Until 21 June the Sun will be drifting along in the airy sign of Gemini, the area of your chart devoted to health, daily routine and work, none of which is going to be particularly exciting but we can't have fireworks every month now, can we? Mind you, you can get a great deal done on the professional front, so put your head down and get on with it.

From 22 June onwards the Sun will be in Cancer, your opposite number, so the focus seems to be on partnerships, both professional and personal. You'll find it a great deal easier to get on with other people, for a change, instead of being suspicious of their motives and wondering if they're trying to 'steal a march on you'. Nothing could be further from the truth; if you want any help all you've got to do is ask, so make sure that you do.

Mercury will be drifting along in Gemini all month, so there are bound to be minor changes where work matters are concerned, and perhaps, too, some new members of staff. Extend the hand of friendship because you don't want to make enemies when all's said and done. It might be a good idea to rest up from time to time, because you could be out-stripping yourself and finishing up exhausted. See that you don't.

Venus will be in Cancer until 14 June, so you've got a couple of weeks when all your relationships and other people in your life, both rivals and loved ones, are in high spirits. Furthermore, if you happen to be fancy-free, this might be the time when you'll meet someone worthwhile, so keep your eyes peeled, won't you?

After 14 June Venus will be moving into Leo, the area of your chart devoted to those you are financially dependent upon, as well as club activity. All of these could bring good luck as well as, perhaps, romance. The only thing you need to do is to keep your eyes peeled, so hopefully you're going to do just that.

Mars will be in Cancer all month. Once more the focus is on relationships. There will be times when you're not just looking for love, but more for physical gratification – most unlike you, but then you are human after all, as others will suddenly observe and appreciate, so don't hold back, just be a little bit careful.

℞

The pattern made by the stars focuses on other people's wants and needs this month. If you are prepared to give and take, then you'll not only be making new contacts and new friends, but also new lovers too – always assuming, of course, you already haven't got someone tucked away. In the main, then, it's going to be a useful and happy time, so make sure that you make the most of it, won't you?

Lastly, make sure that you take into consideration other people's wants and needs. If you can do this, this should be a very happy and contented month.

1 SATURDAY You seem to be faced with a situation which demands confidence and application, both of which you generally have. However, you may feel it's an unfair test which presses all of your Capricorn buttons and produces an overwhelming desire to do a swift about-turn. Yet you have everything to gain and nothing to lose by rising to the bait. This is your chance to prove that you have the flair, determination and talent to succeed.

2 SUNDAY Time simply isn't on your side today, but you can't afford to procrastinate any further. Doing so puts at risk a relationship or a project that has its flaws, but is basically sound and good. Try not to demand too much of other people and, most of all, remember that they, like you, have their shortcomings. As someone born in Capricorn you know only too well there's no light without darkness, although one is easier to accept than the other.

3 MONDAY Today Uranus will be going into retrograde movement. Unfortunately this is in the financial area of your chart, so for every step you take forward, you'll need to take two backwards. Unexpected expenses may drain your resources far more than you would have anticipated. Try to stay calm, though, this matter will right itself in the fullness of time. All you've got to do is wait, and you've got bags of patience, haven't you?

4 TUESDAY It is likely that you are feeling more confident and secure, and in the next few weeks you will be forming new relationships and ties which will support you and your ideas for some time to come. Regarding old alliances, it is likely that you will have to decide fairly soon whether you can cope with them, whether they are necessary. If not, it may be time to make a change.

5 WEDNESDAY You may be expecting far too much out of a current problem or job. Unusually, it looks as if you are look- ing for the easy way out, although subconsciously you know there simply isn't one. Possibly this aspect is making you lazy, in which case it might be a good idea to stick to routine and save those world-shattering decisions (in any area of life) for another day, when you're seeing things more clearly.

6 THURSDAY Guard against being too clever by half, which at any rate would be unusual for you. You're going to be greatly tempted to try and get away with something, but you'll be caught out if you do. This is a splendid time for meeting new friends and acquaintances, though you may not be able to keep these friendships for long for some reason.

7 FRIDAY The stars today could create a certain amount of insecurity or uncertainty where work matters are concerned. Don't panic, Capricorn; after all, you have a couple of days to think about it. Just stick to routine today and use the next couple of days for trying to work out what your next move should be. It will become apparent to you once you really relax, because whenever you are stressed out it does tend to impair your judgement.

8 SATURDAY Today Mercury decides to see sense and move into direct movement once more, so from here on in you need not worry about signing on the dotted line, going to interviews or mixing with people born under the sign of Virgo or Gemini. Furthermore, those of you embroiled in a legal matter should find that all will come out on your side in the end. All you need is self-belief.

9 SUNDAY There could be a career change in connection with sport, romance and children. You should welcome this with open arms – after all, Capricorn, although you would like events and people to be set in stone, this just isn't possible. The world must keep spinning and you must keep changing. It's the same for all of us, and the sooner you accept this fact, the better.

10 MONDAY You must make sure that other people are in a position to be able to appreciate you for what you are, and not for what they are trying to make you. Providing the dead wood has been cut out of your life, you will be finding more security and contentment. However, it is likely that you are still wrestling with a financial problem, and because of this you may have to make a settlement which could deplete your resources for a while. Nevertheless, once this has been done you will be heaving a sigh of relief.

11 TUESDAY Today the stars are making you much more adaptable and ready to make changes and open up your head to other people's ideas and suggestions. Those of you who are travelling are sure to be very successful, and paperwork has a touch of magic about it too. This evening your long-made plans may change, but you'll be able to 'go with the flow' and enjoy yourself regardless.

12 WEDNESDAY Dangers seem to be inevitable today. There could also be some exciting news which sets your household into frantic activity. Maybe somebody is coming home and you want to make the right impression. If not, it may be a case of entertaining a few friends and wanting to get it right – you perfectionist, you.

13 THURSDAY Don't worry, Capricorn, today you will achieve what you set out to accomplish, but only by keeping your emotions under strict control. Luckily, this is something you have no difficulty with. Mind you, this does not mean that you have to accept changes which will harm your long-term interests, but you must remember not to answer angry words with bitter retorts – your reply could very well cause an unpleasant quarrel.

14 FRIDAY Other people on the professional front will help you to realize that you have at last turned a corner where a particular problem or puzzle is concerned. Unseen obstacles in your way, while frustrating, are only temporary. Bide your time and don't be tempted to take unnecessary or potentially costly risks, because if you do, you will regret it. This evening, try to get out and about with people you don't know that well, because discovering what makes them tick will keep you fascinated for hours.

15 SATURDAY Venus will be moving into the fiery sign of Leo, the area of your chart devoted to big business and, to a degree, team effort. If you're in the middle of litigation or have created some sort of muddle which needs sorting out by a 'legal beagle', then this is the day for doing just that. Don't just sit at home chewing your fingernails, that will accomplish precious little.

16 SUNDAY You will get about as far as you can in one particular direction, then you will need to retrace your steps before you can progress again. Delays and frustrations might mean that someone else could temporarily get ahead of you. Never mind, your turn will come soon and you will then be able to catch up in no uncertain fashion. This evening you may feel guilty about enjoying yourself, especially if you are being entertained by someone who is temporarily out of pocket.

17 MONDAY It's a time for shopping for special items, but remember that your high spirits could lead you into spending more than you can realistically afford. It may be boring, but even so it's a good idea to take along a list and stick to it religiously because, in this way, you'll be able to end the day in a solvent state rather than completely down on your uppers.

18 TUESDAY Be careful not to upset other people, or a relationship could come to a grinding halt. Mind you, if you're looking for an excuse to exclude somebody from your life, the stars are providing you with one at this time. However, in the main it's always wisest to plan before leaping into action, because to do the latter often leads to regret, something you find difficult to live with.

19 WEDNESDAY There may be a slowing-down of activities, but this will work in your favour in the long run, particularly where money matters are concerned, so don't grumble too loudly. The influence of a superior or more experienced person will certainly be useful when trying to solve a thorny personal problem. The only question is, can you step out of your Capricorn character and be a little more confiding? It's entirely up to you.

20 THURSDAY The stars may lead you into considering some kind of self-improvement, either physically or mentally. Well, you always aim for perfection, don't you, Capricorn? Whichever you decide upon, the decision is likely to be a good one as you will find a new, interesting and more stimulating image and will feel more confident about yourself all round. If you're involved in foreign affairs, you can expect a great deal of change and plenty of news.

21 FRIDAY All work can be done today. You can turn your attention to details and even routine without so much as stifling a yawn. Yes, a plodding mood seems to have overwhelmed you and this, of course, is always useful for clearing the decks, both on the work front and at home. It allows you to start afresh, and that's something members of your sign are good at doing, throwing out the old order in order to take on the new.

22 SATURDAY Today the Sun will be moving into Cancer, your opposite number. All relationships should be flourishing and everybody is co-operative, which makes a nice pleasant change, doesn't it? Take advantage of this and don't plod on alone.

23 SUNDAY A vibrant sociable mood colours this day; it's a time when you'll find it relatively easy to find support and affection. Your enthusiasm is great, but you need to keep your feet on the ground. Colleagues and friends will very easily become sparring partners, but that's how you like it, it keeps the sparks flying. This evening you'll be highly susceptible to outside influences, so don't let flattery deceive you. Mind you, there's a distinct possibility that one of your idealized heroes could very well fall off their pedestal at some point today.

24 MONDAY You need to think long and hard about career moves. Try to put recent changes and new opportunities into their proper perspective. It may very well be that an intense relationship is disturbing your equilibrium; even so, you mustn't turn down the chance of a little excitement. New friends that you meet will make you think deeply, especially where issues over controlling money are concerned. All areas of life require a certain amount of diplomacy today, so see if you can nip down to the shops and buy an ounce or two.

25 TUESDAY Wise management of time and energy is important now, mainly due to the fact that any imbalance may affect your health. Your creative talents will be appreciated and you can inspire support from colleagues. Intense, open confrontation with a loved one will stir your passions when really you should be using objectivity and flexibility. Do your best to guard against woolly, impractical thinking and, if you can manage to do so, the day can end on an affectionate and lively note.

β

26 WEDNESDAY This is a fine time for mixing business with pleasure. Loved ones and colleagues will get on with you like a house on fire. Discussing your ambitions and professional desires in the comfort of your own home will make you be seen in a much softer light. You may even be able to turn a potential rival into an ally.

27 THURSDAY You're full of confidence and get up and go. This is a day to use really well, Capricorn, so don't hang back where your ambitions are concerned. You're filled with a solar light and power, so that others are easily impressed by what you have to say and what you do. Naturally, this will reflect well on your love life, where you prove to be irresistible.

28 FRIDAY Do make certain that you can cover your expenses and, if not, don't build up more credit than you can realistically afford. Hopefully, you're a typical Capricorn, in which case it will be relatively easy for you to avoid this foolish pitfall. This evening, opt for inexpensive entertainments – after all, it's who you're with that counts, not how much you spend.

29 SATURDAY Money that's owed comes rolling in, and not only that, but it will also be easy for you to generate more. If ever there was a time for presenting your ideas and suggestions to loved ones, this is it. Once you have their seal of approval, you will feel more confident about letting your professional contacts know what's going on between those ears of yours. Well, let's face it, you can be secretive.

30 SUNDAY Today you find it difficult to sit still. Whether you're at home or at work, you're making plenty of phone calls and catching up on all the gossip, and perhaps making social arrangements for the future. By the time this day is through you'll realize it wasn't a madly important one, but at least it was satisfying – and that's something, let's face it.

JULY

Until 22 July the Sun will be drifting through the watery sign of Cancer, your opposite number. Other people are going to be confident, full of good ideas and also ready to listen to yours, which makes a pleasant change, doesn't it? Don't try to knock other people down though, if you're in a bad mood. That wouldn't be fair. Instead, try to go along with their high spirits and you'll feel a good deal better.

From 23 July onwards, the Sun will be drifting along in the fiery sign of Leo, the area of your chart devoted to people you're financially dependent upon, banking matters, and insurance. This doesn't seem to be very exciting in a general way, certainly if you observe the daily guide (below) you'll be able to pick your way through to a much more exciting time, so see what you can do.

During the first week of July, Mercury will be in Gemini. Lots of minor changes will be going on where work matters are concerned. The only problem is, if you're feeling a little under the weather it would be a good idea to be kind to yourself, because small health irritations can become more serious if you neglect yourself – not a very clever thing to do.

On 7 July, Mercury will be moving into Cancer, your opposite number. There will be lots of new people entering your life, and those who are already there will have lots of little changes they want to make; some of these will involve short-distance travel. Don't be an old stick in the mud, be a little bit more adventurous and be prepared for anything 'new'.

On the 26th, Mercury moves on into Leo, where it will stay for the rest of the month. You may be asked to travel because of work, or take extra work home with you. Do resist this if you can, because it would only be a drain on your energy.

Venus will be coasting along in Leo until 10 July, in the area of your chart devoted to banking matters, those you are financially dependent upon, and big business, especially insurance. If this applies to you, you've got a good time for pushing ahead with all of your desires. For other Capricorns, you may suddenly become attracted to a Leo, but the relationship is likely to be short-lived.

From 11 July Venus will be moving through Virgo, the area of your chart devoted to further education, long-distance travel and the affairs of foreigners. Stay alert for strange-sounding accents, in your personal life or your professional, because they are likely to be extremely lucky for you.

Mars will be situated in your opposite sign of Cancer up until 13 July, so there could be some tension in your relationships, especially those that have been around for a while. Somebody's got to be sensible and it might as well be you, Capricorn, because possibly nobody else is going to.

On 14 July Mars will be moving into Leo, where it stays for the remainder of the month. There could be some tension on the work front through no fault of your own. If you work as part of a team, though, of course you will have to take your share of any kind of blame, but don't be overly anxious to do so – don't ever volunteer.

The pattern made by the stars suggests that people at work could be grumpy, bad-tempered and blame you for things that go wrong. Actually you'll feel indignant about this and you should stand up for yourself – but do so with abundant charm, rather than aggression or abrasiveness, otherwise you will not be very popular, I can assure you.

1 MONDAY It's certainly going to be an active day, with your career and your role at work being highlighted. If you're experiencing frustrations and obstacles where team work is concerned, you'll know the right way to handle them on this particular day – impartial discussions will be particularly useful. This evening it's possible that you'll be acting the role of dictator at home – for some reason or other you're not inclined to be flexible – but believe it or not, Capricorn, you will invite more co-operation and assistance by adopting a humble attitude. This may also help stalemated plans to move ahead once more.

2 TUESDAY An explosive individual seems to be influencing your thinking. It's a good time, though, to discuss long-range plans, not overlooking practical needs and limitations. Make sure that you keep to your personal goals and obligations, or you'll be unpopular at home. Horizons continue to expand on all levels; you must be ready to take advantage of this.

3 WEDNESDAY You have a touch of magic about you today, which will be felt where work is concerned. Your originality will impress everyone around you and they'll be anxious to help you out in any way they can. On a more personal level, you're attracting new friends, contacts and lovers like moths to a flame. If you already have a partner, for heaven's sake take care, because there's only so much they're prepared to put up with, and who can blame them? You should be able to understand, Capricorn.

ƥ

4 THURSDAY Today you'll be making some professional decisions. You do so with a certain amount of panache, style and common sense. This evening an older person will be handing on some useful advice, whether you choose to listen or not is entirely up to you, but it might be a good idea to do so because even you have a great deal to learn in life.

5 FRIDAY Your mental energy is certainly increased by the stars today. You may be drawn unexpectedly to witticisms, and although you are more impulsive in speech than writing, this will be controllable. You have the ability to study and put long-made ideas and plans into action. Energetic, intellectual conditions are looking good when it comes to the realization of your hopes and wishes.

6 SATURDAY The stars today emphasize lighthearted and more enjoyable aspects of living. When it comes to romance, you're ridiculously flirty, even if you do have a partner and, if this is the case, there's sure to be tears before bedtime. On the other hand, if you're single, you're spoiled for choice. Don't make any decisions for the time being – well, not until you've had a chance to get to know new people a little better – to rush in would be foolhardy and also asking for a broken heart.

7 SUNDAY Today Mercury will be moving into the watery sign of Cancer, your opposite number. There are going to be new people entering your life, and you'll certainly be enjoying their company. It's going to be a good time if you're involved in legal matters or travel; such affairs are well starred so you can be confident. Therefore, push ahead.

8 MONDAY Wherever you go, other people seem to be more gentle, creative and receptive to your hopes and wishes, so this is certainly the time for asking for one or two favours; they'll be granted without a second thought. And, if you are unattached, an invitation to a party should not be ignored, because it could lead to an important romance. All in all, then, plenty to look forward to at this time.

9 TUESDAY Try as you might, you simply can't pin others down to saying 'yes' or 'no.' Never mind, a pleasant 'good morning' will have to do. The best thing to do is to keep yourself to yourself and wait for this mood to pass. Don't do anything important.

10 WEDNESDAY The stars are certainly livening up your relationships. The only problem is that certain loved ones will be hypersensitive, so you'll need to watch what you say and what you do, unless, of course, you don't give a jot about cutting them to the quick. If you're fancy-free, there'll be a chance for you to meet new people which should be snapped up, because although the relationships may be impermanent they are certainly going to be a great deal of fun while they last. Contact from an old friend surprises you.

11 THURSDAY Today Venus will be going into Virgo and the area of your life which rules matters related to far-off places, foreigners and legal matters. But some of you may be falling head-over-heels with somebody with a strange accent. You may find this stimulating, but hopefully the attraction goes a little bit deeper than this, otherwise it's not going to last for very long, that's for sure.

12 FRIDAY The stars stir up a certain amount of insecurity, and you're beginning to wonder whether somebody you rely on financially is going to be able to meet their end of the expenses. There's no point in worrying yourself into a nervous wreck; contact the person concerned, sit them down and have a good serious conversation, but on no account become arrogant or start issuing ultimatums because, as a Capricorn, you could be playing your own worst enemy and I don't think that's very clever, do you?

13 SATURDAY It's quite possible that you may be tempted into eating or drinking more than you should; while some of you may get away with it, others may be causing a tragedy or, at the very least, finish up out of pocket. If you must go gadding about, make arrangements either to sleep over or to arrange a lift at the end of the evening. This is infinitely preferable to turning this day into one you'll never forget, for all the wrong reasons.

14 SUNDAY Today Mars will be moving into the fiery sign of Leo, the area of your chart devoted to the financial affairs of other people, insurance and perhaps team effort too. Mind you, all these areas will be tense, the fur could be flying, but luckily, as a Capricorn you are a patient person and, therefore, it is you who will have to take control before other people do something they regret.

15 MONDAY Possibly somebody will be interesting you in a new spare-time activity, and you're wondering whether or not to take it more seriously at some point in the future. Give yourself time before coming to any kind of hasty conclusion, otherwise you may live to regret it.

♑

16 TUESDAY This is certainly a good time for those of you involved with creativity and sport, because you've loads of energy to spare right now. Other Capricorns will be throwing themselves 100% into the social scene and flirting outrageously with anything that walks. Just make sure you don't pursue the boss' lover, or give chase to someone who couldn't be less interested, because that could prove to be a tremendous blow to your fierce pride. If you already have a partner, it might be a good idea to take them along as bodyguard.

17 WEDNESDAY You may hear of a new project or fresh contract which is going to make the rest of the year particularly important. Whichever applies, you'll be feeling more secure on a professional level and won't be able to wait to get home and tell your loved one this evening. If you're fancy-free, you'll be more attracted to those with something going on between their ears than with merely a pretty face or a fine pair of shoulders. Yes, Capricorn, you're really digging beneath the surface here.

18 THURSDAY It looks as if you'll be keeping a high profile. Hopefully it's because you've been a clever Goat, and not because you've drunk too much at lunchtime and are making a complete idiot of yourself. Try to concentrate excess energy into finishing up work, otherwise there may be a mad dash a little bit later on when you could make serious mistakes, which may only be discovered at a later date.

19 FRIDAY The success of this particular day relies largely on your ability to co-operate with other people as well as accepting the fact that we all need a little help some time. Naturally, you're fiercely competitive and something of a loner, but if you are to get through what needs to be done, you'll welcome an extra pair of hands. This evening there may be something special going on at a club, in which case you should go – not only will it lead to romance, but to a thoroughly enjoyable opportunity to let off steam.

20 SATURDAY Friends and contacts seem to be constantly on the phone to you during this particular day; maybe they're vying for your company which, of course, is most flattering. Whatever applies, it might be a good idea to take some time to discuss where you should be going, and with whom, for fear of making a mistake and also, of course, because you might have a partner who would appreciate consultation. After all, you'd be the first to complain if somebody made plans and automatically assumed that you would go along with them. So give somebody else the same courtesy.

21 SUNDAY The stars suggest you reach out into life and make a few changes. This would be an ideal time for changing your image, or perhaps your hairstyle; the impact this makes could be quite outstanding. You'll also be thinking about taking up a new course of learning at some time in the future, or perhaps a new leisure-time activity. Whichever applies here, this is certainly going to be a stimulating and interesting time.

22 MONDAY Today Mercury will be moving into Leo, the area of your chart devoted to insurance matters, work and legal affairs. All of these should go in your favour, just as long as you don't spread yourself too thinly. As far as possible, concentrate your energies.

℞

23 TUESDAY Today you're much softer in your approach to other people, which is just as well considering they're rushed off their feet. Certainly, if you're going to any kind of important meeting you'll be the centre of attention and, if you are single, you'll be noticing several admirers. But if you're taking a loved one along with you, because the occasion may be also social, don't give in to the temptation to dump them on the sidelines while you mingle, trying to get as much action as you possibly can – naughty, naughty.

24 WEDNESDAY Today is the day of the full Moon, and it occurs in the airy sign of Aquarius. This is no time for new beginnings or for being at all daring. Remember that this is the area of your chart devoted to money, so hang on to your little valuables because they could go astray, or even be lifted by somebody unscrupulous. As always, during a full Moon it is not a good idea to make any kind of fresh start, so stick to routine, that's the clever way to go.

25 THURSDAY Well, your day is sure to be a good one. You're ready to give as much as you possibly can to other people without any thought of gaining anything in return. This is just the right attitude right now. No doubt, because of your mood, you'll be planning some kind of social arrangement for the future; others will be happy to allow you to take the lead, which is nice.

26 FRIDAY You'll certainly have a wonderful time if you're participating in any kind of sport, but if you're expected to stay at home and behave yourself, some tension and stress may develop. Do anything to rid yourself of this mood, because you don't want to spoil other people's day. A brisk walk, for example, may do the trick.

ß

27 SATURDAY This seems to be a good day; everything is running smoothly for a change. If on the other hand you are at home, many of you may be tempted to go to the nearby shops and spend far too much. Luckily, though, you will retain your common sense, and so are unlikely to go completely 'potty'. You'll buy only that which is absolutely necessary. If you want a day for making up with somebody you may have upset recently, this is the one to choose.

28 SUNDAY Today you are advised to keep your purse or wallet tucked safe underneath your bed, lest you give in to a mad, extravagant mood. The phone is likely to be hectic, with many chances to have fun in connection with some kind of celebration. You're positively spoiled for choice, but if you have a partner you may have to sit down with them and decide exactly what you're going to do so that you don't upset other people.

29 MONDAY The stars are providing the oil for the wheels of your mind, and you're coming up with some interesting ideas for the future which will be greatly appreciated and applauded by others. Do get out as much as you possibly can, because fresh faces will be stimulating and may even be useful at a later date – and, let's face it Capricorn, you're not one to look a gift horse in the mouth now, are you?

30 TUESDAY This particular day, whatever you undertake, you'll be making sure that it runs smoothly, and so by the time the day is through you'll have a smile on your face and possibly the gratitude of others, too. Lastly, make sure that you give plenty of attention to that special person in your life, otherwise you'll feel bad about yourself – and indeed, so will they.

ß

31 WEDNESDAY You'll probably find it difficult to remember the last time you were in a strong enough position to call the shots and influence events, either in your emotional life or at work. With the planetary activity in your chart, you shouldn't be afraid to ask for what you want; you may get it a great deal sooner than you could possibly hope. This evening be sure you're out locally – somebody you meet by chance could put a good thing your way, possibly romantically but more likely connected with your ambitions.

AUGUST

Until 22 August the Sun will be drifting along in the fiery sign of Leo, the area of your chart devoted to other people's money, banking and perhaps team effort too. This is not a time to isolate yourself; if you do you may miss out on the chance to improve yourself, either in your personal life or maybe in your professional.

On 23 August the Sun will be moving into Virgo, the area of your chart devoted to matters related to far-off places, legal affairs, insurance matters and your lofty ambitions. Don't let anybody hold you back at this time, because if you do you will seriously miss out and you'll be blaming everybody else when the person you should be looking to can be found in the mirror.

During the first week of this month, Mercury will be in Leo. You may be signing an important contract. This aside, should you be a parent, then children will be extremely lively and you'll be drawing closer to them.

On 6 August Mercury will be moving into Virgo, the area of your chart devoted to matters related to higher education, foreign affairs and perhaps your high ideals. You can make a great deal of progress at this time, all you need is some added confidence, so look in the mirror each day and tell yourself you're as good as anybody else – because, let's face it, you are.

Venus will be in Virgo until 7 August. This is at the zenith of your chart, making it an exciting time for romance and relationships. Also, if you are looking for a new job, there could be one just around the corner.

Venus will be moving into Libra on the 8th. For the majority of the month, work matters will have a happy, contented glow about them. Furthermore, if your work is at all creative or artistic, you'll be doing exceptionally well and getting lots of pats on the back. The only pitfall could be that you may also combine business with romance, which is all very well if you are single but, if not, there's going to be some trouble, so behave yourself.

Mars will be in Leo until 29 August, so it is important that you stick to the letter of the law because if you imagine you can get away with anything, either the traffic laws or any other kind of lawbreaking, I'm afraid you're going to be very disappointed and this could ruin your time, so be your usual, sensible Capricorn self and you'll have precious little to worry about.

The pattern made by the stars suggests that you're going to be much more outgoing. Furthermore, you will begin many new projects and relationships in your life, but it is essential that you see everything and everyone through to a conclusion, otherwise loose ends hanging around could prove to trip you up at a later date. Try to bear this in mind.

1 THURSDAY The old grey matter is certainly whizzing around these days, it's a wonder you don't have steam coming out of your ears. Your brain is full to bursting with no end of original thoughts, any of which could make you a good deal richer and more fulfilled in future. Even so, there is a limit to the amount of support you can expect from other people, especially work colleagues and employers. Mind you, as a Capricorn you prefer to carve out your own fate anyway, so this is unlikely to faze you one little bit. This evening looks promising for brief encounters.

2 FRIDAY The stars seem to be pulling you in several directions today. They usually urge you to pay what is owing and then move on to something, or maybe even someone, new. However, Capricorn, you know you have to come down to earth, just like the rest of us, once in a while. It would be a good idea not to put this off any longer. Besides, if you get duties out of the way then you'll be able to take advantage of the stars, which are urging you to reach out into life and be more adventurous.

3 SATURDAY This looks as if it's going to be a lively day, and one in which you must be prepared to take advantage of what crops up completely out of the blue. Those closest to you, both within the family and in your friendship circle, are fiercely energetic and highly sexed too. You may have been thinking that this evening would be a good time for resting up, but I'm afraid you won't get much chance to do that.

4 SUNDAY Right now you need a little romance and fun to lighten a serious mood which may have descended. This is a time when you could really afford to be over the top and indulge yourself and those you care about the most. Although there are pressures and demands on your time, there's a strong desire to drop everything and escape from the mundane. Only by letting yourself try something different will you be able to see what gives you the greatest pleasure.

5 MONDAY Other people will be at their most creative, giving and romantic, but at the same time could be a little forgetful or muddled, so if you've any important arrangements it would be worthwhile doing some double-checking, if only to prod the grey matter and remind other people where they're supposed to be at what time.

6 TUESDAY Today Mercury will be moving into Virgo, the area of your chart devoted to higher education, long-distance travel and the affairs of foreigners. This is a day for reaching out into life and to be a little bit more daring. If you can do this, some good things may happen for you, or even to you.

7 WEDNESDAY There may be some good news today in connection with money. All opportunities that cross your path should be considered seriously, no matter how impractical they may seem at first. It's a happy time for you if you work in a big organization, such as the stock exchange, a bank or an insurance firm, and a good time for other Goats who need to meet up with such people to sort out differences – you can win through in the end, Capricorn, you really can.

8 THURSDAY Today is the day of the Full Moon, and it occurs in the fiery sign of Leo. There is the possibility of a promotion or a new challenge in the wind. Grasp this with both hands, because you can do it if you really try. Also, avoid playing the giddy goat by over-indulging. You can channel your good humour in much more positive ways.

9 FRIDAY You could be a little bit snappy, impulsive and rash; these characteristics are best controlled wherever possible. Remember, Capricorn, you're in control of your life, it is not in control of you, or if it is something is seriously wrong. There's no need to give in to negative influences that surround you. Take the helm of your life and steer it along a more steady and reliable course.

10 SATURDAY You'll need to be especially careful and charming when dealing with friends, acquaintances and contacts; they may be rather depressed or in a negative mood, and a cheery word from you will go a long way to cheering them up and making them think more positively. If you've arrangements with other people, especially friends, don't take it for granted that they have remembered to put you in their diary. A little reminder won't do any harm at all.

11 SUNDAY Now you are free to present your ideas to other people, to travel further afield, perhaps in search of work, and also to attend interviews and meetings with much more confidence than you have had for a while. Others will be listening to your ideas and suggestions, and even providing you with a pat on the back. This will certainly help to boost your ego, which is in need of some encouragement.

12 MONDAY Having recently tried to push your life along and probably experiencing something of an uphill struggle, you now feel like opting out of the rat race, at least for a while. Remember, in your imagination you can explore new possibilities and avenues, as well as giving yourself some space to find out what it is you really want out of life. Right now the stars are helping you to see all sides of any situation.

13 TUESDAY Because of your active head, you sometimes find it difficult to keep pace with your own ideas. Today, the stars seem to suggest that you will have a chance to realize a dream. However, the more you try, the less you will achieve, so try to trim down your activities and concentrate on your most inventive and imaginative ideas.

14 WEDNESDAY It looks as if you need to reshuffle your life in order to satisfy your growing need for excitement. Recently, security has been your all-important goal, but now you feel like exploring beyond familiar faces and places. Remember, any side of life which has become stale needs only one person to change it, so take matters into your own hands. What is needed now is a change of scenery.

15 THURSDAY This is a time for making a real effort to realize one of your ambitions, and certainly to keep a high profile on the work front, because this will be attracting good luck to you. Your ability to communicate is always strong, of course, but now you are expressing yourself in the most imaginative and quirky way, which will not only amuse other people, but will also get the message across in no uncertain fashion.

16 FRIDAY Today it will be all too easy for you to over-react to excitement and indulge in a certain amount of extravagance. Yes, it looks as if you're in a mood to take risks, but if you give in to this today, you will have to come down to earth with a bump tomorrow and account for your actions.

17 SATURDAY Your behaviour is somewhat erratic and so, if you have social arrangements, you'd be wise to do a bit of double-checking, because other people's lives seem to be packed full of action and they may totally (unintentionally) overlook you – don't take this to heart. If you need any favours, pick your moment carefully and you'll find them willingly granted.

18 SUNDAY The stars are encouraging you to widen your field of experience and perhaps take on a fresh line of study. Someone important who lives far away in a different country, is likely to be getting in touch with you over the next few days or so. You're at your most idealistic, but you need to apply a certain amount of practicality, otherwise you'll be floating around the stratosphere, no doubt enjoying yourself but accomplishing precious little.

19 MONDAY Today it looks as if your friends understand that this is a decisive phase at work, and you now need a good deal of support if you are to win through. Follow their words and act upon them, because this is a great time for making carefully planned moves. Your love life will also compensate for these difficulties, so concentrate on the future.

20 TUESDAY The stars are helping you to broaden your horizons. Because of this, many of you will be making plans to take a trip in the not too distant future. Lady Luck can be found in the company of those with fascinating names and accents. Many of you will become seriously emotionally involved with those who come from different parts of the world, and this will give you a good deal to think about.

21 WEDNESDAY Avoid making any financial decisions, because there is a real danger of you failing to take into consideration all salient points. If you rush where angels fear to tread, you are sure to regret it at a later date. Ideally, use this day for putting the finishing touches to work or making plans for the future.

22 THURSDAY Today is the day of the full Moon, and it falls in the airy sign of Aquarius, the area of your chart devoted to money. Oh dear! It looks as if some of that nasty stuff is going to go to waste, either that or someone will be lifting one of your precious possessions when you're not looking and you'll feel very sad about this. Be watchful and you can avoid this outcome.

23 FRIDAY Today the Sun will be moving into the earthy sign of Virgo, the area of your chart devoted to matters related to far-off places. If you have a loved one, or other friend, in foreign climes they are likely to be either on the phone or writing to you. Either way, you will be extremely pleased. If you've a Virgo in your life, they're going to be much more confident from here on in.

24 SATURDAY Today there is a natural tendency for you to chop and change your mind several times throughout the day where important matters are concerned. If you really find yourself caught on the thorns of a dilemma, get a piece of paper and write down a list of pros and cons and see which proves the longer. This will help you to be more practical as well as pushing you into the right direction, which can be no bad thing.

25 SUNDAY If you have made plans, and they were made some time ago, it would be a good idea to get on the telephone and double-check, in case other people have completely forgotten, which is a strong possibility. When it comes to the personal side of life, you're more interested in fulfilling your sexual needs than becoming embroiled in a steamy romance. If you already have a partner, they are likely to be seriously chased during the evening. However, it's unlikely that they will be running too fast.

26 MONDAY There's a strong chance that you are quickly gaining confidence in your ability to improve your life from every angle. Certainly, there are some financial considerations that can't be decided just yet, but at least you're beginning to feel that your difficulties are not immovable. In fact, being your usual flexible and open self, you will be attracting new opportunities which will help you to win through at a later date.

27 TUESDAY The stars will increase your gift for logic and persuasion, and help to offset the confusing influences that may be surrounding you. Most importantly of all, you must not waver or wobble. Believe in your own ability to know when something is right. A personal relationship, or perhaps a close friend or colleague, will offer you the chance to enhance your lifestyle in some way.

28 WEDNESDAY A great deal is taking place in your world at this time, and much of the activity is largely as a result of other people's actions. They may have the whip hand, but there are also great benefits to be had from being co-operative. This is a time when you need others to help you realize your dreams and interests, and to bring greater scope into your life.

29 THURSDAY The stars today are helping you to reach as high as you can towards your ambitions. Between now and the end of the year, you must make the most of chances that are lying in wait, because they will help to smooth your path in a real way. So, if ever there was a time for rowing out the boat of ambition, this is it. Whether your goal or objective is professional or purely personal, chase it wholeheartedly.

30 FRIDAY Although there are a few questions which need answering in connection with your status and position, what you have to remember is that, without change, everything is not only dull and boring, but stagnant. So don't be shaken by current upheavals; see them as a chance to bring greater opportunities to develop as a person. Certainly the stars are inspiring you with a greater ability to learn from past mistakes.

31 SATURDAY Today is likely to bring unexpected changes into your life. Mind you, change is one of your favourite words and so, no doubt, you'll be ready to embrace it whenever you feel fit. Luckily, it looks as if you have done your homework, for a change, and so, when the time is right, you'll be able to push into life in a big way.

SEPTEMBER

Until 22 September the Sun will be drifting through Virgo, the area of your chart devoted to higher education, long-distance travel and legal affairs. Any or all of these can be pushed with alacrity and confidence in the knowledge that you're doing the right thing. Of course, that's always important.

On the 23rd the Sun will be moving into Libra, the zenith point of your chart. You're going to be working extremely hard, for once Capricorn is galvanized into action you are unstoppable, aren't you? You most certainly are. However, do try to paint on a wider canvas, all work and no play doesn't make you very attractive to those around you.

Mercury will be in Libra all month, therefore on the work front there are going to be minor changes, perhaps lots of meetings in which you'll play a prominent role. If there are new members of staff, greet them warmly – it's better to make a friend than a potential enemy, I think you'll agree. If you've a Gemini or a Virgo at work, it would be a good idea to defer to them if you feel any confusion or hesitation.

Venus will be in Libra during the first seven days of the month. Once more, this is the zenith point of your chart and you're going to be socializing much more than is usually the case where professional matters are concerned. Furthermore, if your job is artistic you will impress many people, including your good self.

On 8 September Venus will be moving into Scorpio, the area of your chart devoted to friends and contacts. When in doubt it would be a good idea to defer to them. Furthermore, you may be joining a new club, and for some of you there may be some luck where romance is concerned. All in all, this looks to be an enjoyable time.

Mars will be in Virgo all month. There could be some stresses and strains where foreign affairs – and, indeed, for-eigners – are concerned. Make sure that you stay polite and conciliatory during this period, otherwise you'll live to regret it in a very big way, I can assure you.

The pattern made by the stars is a rather scattered one, suggesting that you may be taking too much onto those narrow shoulders. If you can delegate a little bit, not only will you win the confidence and respect of others, but you'll be making things a good deal easier on yourself. You don't want to go home in the evenings bad-tempered and ready for a fight. If you do that, you'll ruin a potentially good month and will be kicking yourself for quite some time, I can assure you.

Lastly, there is a certain amount of luck waiting for you; all you have to do is discover it. This could come from a fire sign in your circle, therefore look for an Aries, Leo or Sagittarius: they'll be willing to help you with any queries you may have, and you'll be doing the right thing, believe you me.

1 SUNDAY A financial weight has been lifted off your shoulders. But this doesn't mean you can become extravagant. Wilder dreams and schemes are on your mind, and certain planetary influences are giving you more hope and less disbelief. Now is your chance to plot and build something stable. Just don't give up on being the first to think of it.

2 MONDAY Obstacles are slowly being broken down in your private affairs. The planets can help you create an efficient way to get yourself and others motivated. If they don't see it, then give them time. You're not normally impatient, but sometimes the thrill of change is more compelling than the status quo.

3 TUESDAY At last, someone appears to be on your wavelength. It's not that they were ever out of step, only unsure whether your feelings were genuine or not. The planets are giving you an opportunity to persuade other people that you're serious. Just take care you don't get too carried away in the heat of the moment.

4 WEDNESDAY Waiting with baited breath for a change of fortune has been exhausting. But gradually, due to the planets' influence, you can sigh with relief instead of gasping for air. The only obstacle now to making your life more comfortable is self-doubt. It's not that you have to take risks. Remember, where there is continuity, you can be sure of security.

5 THURSDAY Professionally you can now judge when to create a favourable image of yourself. But you're still confused by someone else's ploy. Reject their antics as merely over-sensitive to your growing reputation. The planets are giving you the chance to work at your ambitions. But also make others realize you're worth every minute of their time.

6 FRIDAY You can make important financial decisions today under favourable circumstances. You may also meet up with somebody who has an excellent financial suggestion which you should at least be prepared to consider. When it comes to having fun today, you are likely to opt for quieter pleasures because your nerves are beginning to jangle a bit. Therefore, be careful with whom you spend your time.

7 SATURDAY Today is the day of the new Moon, and it occurs in the earthy sign of Virgo, the area of your chart devoted to matters related to far-off places, higher education and legal matters. Any or all of these can be pushed like crazy, so don't let the grass grow beneath your feet otherwise you will be reproaching yourself for quite some time.

8 SUNDAY Today Venus will be moving into the watery sign of Scorpio, the area of your life devoted to friends, acquaintances and contacts in general, as well as team effort. All of these matters, or perhaps just some of them, will have a rosy glow about them and you can proceed with confidence, so do not hesitate.

9 MONDAY Deep within you've guessed for some time that new experiences are lurking around the corner. Although it's no surprise that someone's being ambivalent about the future, you now have little choice but to hint at your plans. Perhaps what they have ignored is what needs to be addressed. That way you can both begin to access your wildest dreams.

10 TUESDAY Previously hidden ideas are suddenly being revealed. They seem like awfully good ventures which you can't overlook – especially as for some time you've felt the need to make some kind of shift in your outlook. Conventional aspects of how to behave have taken up a lot of your time. But now radical moves are necessary in order to make personal progress. Over the next few days, make sure you capitalize on your visions and turn them into reality.

11 WEDNESDAY There seems to be a new twist to an old plan, and it suddenly appears much more viable to continue an association rather than drop it altogether. You're at a point where a graceful compromise has been reached without you being aware of it. The stars today are expansive and you can now modify your venture, and know where you are truly heading.

12 THURSDAY Clarification of what you want from a certain relationship is becoming accessible, thanks to the planets. All those feelings and thoughts you've been denying are being magnified before your eyes. Communicate, and don't put it off any longer. You are too enthusiastic about love to let go of something real.

℞

13 FRIDAY Strangely, it feels as if you can bring to life any stifled creative issues. However inhibited you've felt recently, it's time to express your desires. Fooling yourself that you don't need certain romantic pursuits is one thing, but don't deny yourself the pleasure that could be yours. Take a chance and live out a dream.

14 SATURDAY Today Mercury will be going into retrograde movement. While this state of affairs exists it would be most unwise to take unnecessary journeys, to become involved with legal matters at all or to deal (except with caution) with Geminis or Virgos. If you take this advice you'll make life a good deal more enjoyable than it might otherwise be.

15 SUNDAY There's suspense that has surrounded various personal affairs for some time, but gradually the veil is being lifted. Realizing how to change your circumstances is becoming much simpler. Something has to give, and most probably your sense of purpose will propel you into action. Just don't forget that you need to inspire others to be forgiving, too.

16 MONDAY Basically you've been frozen in time, but the stars' animating influence can now get you out of a rut. If others think you're going to extremes, tell them gently you have to live your own life. After all, the original grandeur of your plans is far more realistic now. Modify them a little and you might find people become more supportive.

17 TUESDAY Having already agreed to fit in with other people's plans or ideas, you are now beginning to have second thoughts. Maybe the best thing to do is nothing until you hear from them – but you are far too impatient to wait. At any rate, everything appears to be just fine, and there are a number of options available.

18 WEDNESDAY Among other things, you seem most concerned that others don't interfere in a situation that is already complicated enough. Perhaps you can ask someone else to look into matters on your behalf. Indeed, the chances are that everything has been lined up and, thankfully, once a decision has been made there is no turning back.

19 THURSDAY At first glance it looks as though partners or certain individuals are finally going to meet your needs. Not that you are convinced, as there is always a possibility that they will make things more difficult for you by involving an outsider. Mind you, this could turn out to be a saving grace – rather ironic, don't you think?

20 FRIDAY After recent astrological influences you should start moving along more easily or freely. However, there may be some minor problems or a few irritations which could affect an existing arrangement. At any rate, in this instance your presence isn't required, which is obviously a good sign.

21 SATURDAY Today is the day of the full Moon, occurring in the water sign of Pisces, the area of your chart devoted to short journeys and the mind. If in traffic, stay alert – minor prangs are a possibility here. Furthermore, you may become a little depressed for reasons that are elusive. It might be a good idea to isolate yourself for a couple of hours and sort out your jumbled thoughts. Only then can you really proceed.

ß

22 SUNDAY A time of welcome emotional response, but others may not act with much elegance or remain patient for ever. You could benefit enormously from one association, even if it means being paid off, and you should still receive the same kind of dedication from others as you have come to expect. So at least show some appreciation.

23 MONDAY Today is the day when the Sun will be moving into the airy sign of Libra, the area of your chart devoted to your profession and your work, as well as your relationships with colleagues. You may be working far harder than you have for some time, perhaps in order to catch up. Even so, other people are appreciative of everything you do, and that includes your boss, so do your best to keep at it.

24 TUESDAY Events or situations now taking place may have a bitter-sweet effect. It's difficult to read certain people, as no matter how likable they are, or interested you are, you never quite know how to handle them. Nevertheless, what transpires during this day is worth facing – whether they are on your side or not.

25 WEDNESDAY A perfect link between the stars denotes that others will treat you with much more kindness and consideration than they have of late. Meanwhile, it might be better to insulate yourself from them, but still follow their movements. There's no reason to subject yourself to this torment while things are so chaotic.

26 THURSDAY The stars today could very well alter the balance of your life. Not that this is necessarily a bad thing, because you usually greet the unexpected with open arms, and often surprise developments help you to make the changes you need in order to succeed. So, you should take advantage of any opportunities to go off on a tangent, be with interesting people and generally spread your wings.

27 FRIDAY Those who are closest to you will be more changeable and also more sensitive, so you're not going to get your own way for a change. However, continue to be big-hearted and adaptable, particularly today. There will be an opportunity for you to meet a new circle of friends and this may directly, or indirectly, lead to romance. Grab any chance to make this a 'different' kind of day, because in doing so you'll be able to squeeze as much action out of it as is possible. That's what you need out of life – plenty of movement.

28 SATURDAY This is a time when you are able to draw on past experience to solve any existing complications in your life. Those of you who are unattached may have a loved one abroad. If so, you can be quite sure you'll be hearing from them in the very near future. If you're expected to do any kind of travelling during this period, it will not only be profitable but also enjoyable. Plenty to look forward to, then.

29 SUNDAY What happens now is likely to lead to better conditions and more opportunities in the future. It is up to you to be alert, not only to what is going on on the surface, but behind the scenes. If you want a day for dealing with big business, insurance or tax affairs, you couldn't have a better one than this.

30 MONDAY From now on you may find that relationships with friends, contacts and acquaintances may not be as smooth or as uncomplicated as they have been of late. You'll need to make allowances for the fact that others have their own lives to lead; they can't possibly spend all their time worrying about you. There's a possibility that even your intimates will be more reluctant to confide in you than is usually the case. There's no point in nursing your ill-feelings; not that you could maintain them for any length of time anyway. Simply accept the situation because, like everything else, it will soon come to an end.

OCTOBER

Until 23 October the Sun this month will be drifting along through the air sign of Libra, the area of your chart devoted to prestige, your profession or your job. You may be working hard but don't imagine other people aren't watching. In fact, they may give you extra responsibility if you can cope with it, but please don't take it on board if you feel that you'll have to juggle too many of your interests, otherwise you will become inefficient.

On the 24th the Sun will be moving into Scorpio, the area of your chart devoted to team effort, friendship, acquaintances and perhaps redefining your goals. You have permission from the stars to push ahead with any or all of these, and if you do you'll be operating alongside the stars, who will no doubt help you out quite a lot.

Mercury will be in Virgo from 2 to 10 October, emphasizing matters to do with far-off places. It is a good time for those involved with the import/export business and you are also likely to hear from relations, friends and colleagues who live abroad.

From the 11th Mercury will be occupying Libra, so you may be asked to travel for the sake of your job, or perhaps to sign an important legal document. If the latter should apply, take it along to your local solicitor and get it checked out because, you never know, somebody may be trying to pull the wool over your eyes and you'll feel rather stupid at a later date for having fallen for it.

Venus is in Scorpio all this month, but unfortunately continues its retrograde movement, so where team effort, friends and acquaintances are concerned you need to dig beneath the surface to see what undercurrents are there. If you don't, you'll be setting yourself up for a disappointment or perhaps a hurt, and we really can't have that. If you work as part of a team, don't try to rock the boat – others will be doing plenty of that – just stand by and fulfil your obligations. If others are going to make mistakes, let them do it all on their own.

Mars will be situated in Virgo until the 15th, the area of your chart devoted to team effort, friends and acquaintances. You may be finding it difficult to make an important decision. Try to discover which way to turn. If this is stressing you out, relax for a couple of days and come back to it at a later date, because if you move impulsively now you'll do something that you'll regret for a considerable while, and that would be a great pity, I think you'll agree.

From 16 October until the end of the month, Mars will be in the airy sign of Libra. You may be finding things very hectic on the work front. Try and keep a cool head and don't take things out on friends or colleagues.

The pattern made by the stars is a little scattered this month. Many of the planets are in Libra; if you have a member of this sign in your circle they'll be playing a leading role in what takes place. If you deal with intricate work, try to concentrate a little bit more, because if you don't you could be making a fool of yourself and that would be a great pity.

Lastly, if you feel that you are tense, run-down or just simply exhausted, set aside some time for putting your feet up. You can then return to whatever needs your attention replenished, renewed and, above all else, more optimistic.

1 TUESDAY Today the stars will be encouraging you towards idealism, which is all very well, but when making plans you must consider the practicalities of life, too. Those of you with financial interests abroad will be receiving some happy news, and there may even be cause for celebration which you'll no doubt grab with both hands. This is a good day for making cash decisions, because you're taking all sides of the question into consideration and not operating on superficials only.

2 WEDNESDAY You're at your most idealistic, so heaven help partners and potential co-workers, they're certainly going to have a great deal to live up to. It might be a good idea for you to accept the fact that maybe you're expecting too much. After all, others are only human, as indeed are you. If you can bear this thought in mind, you might be a little easier to approach, and life will be less fraught with disappointment.

3 THURSDAY There's likely to be a temporary change of mood or direction on your part. This is because you're becoming more remote and objective, and also a little bit eccentric and self-absorbed. No doubt you'll make use of these new-found characteristics because you love to throw other people off-balance, it's that mischievous streak in your personality which never changes, no matter how old you grow. Those of you with foreign interests can push them ahead during the days to come.

4 FRIDAY There's certainly a lively feel about the day, and you need to be alert in order to take advantage of a prevailing condition. Prepare for unexpected and eccentric behaviour within your circle of friends. Anything can happen in this area of life, and probably will, but even so you'll be delighted with what occurs and will have no difficulty adapting to it.

5 SATURDAY That grey matter is firing on all cylinders and charisma is oozing out of every pore. Use this day for getting your own way at work, within the family and also in your emotional life. If you're unattached, circulate this evening, because you could be attracting in a big way and you don't want to miss out, that would never do.

6 SUNDAY Today is the day of the new Moon, in the airy sign of Libra, the zenith point of your chart. You have a wonderful day for pushing ahead with your ambitions and also approaching superiors and bosses, who will see you in a good light. Of course, with new Moons it's always a great time for making fresh starts in any area that you choose.

7 MONDAY Mercury has now resumed direct movement, so from here on in you need not fear short journeys, travelling abroad or matters related to the law. Furthermore, Geminis and Virgos who have been in your circle and been something of a 'bug bear' finally calm down and become their usual selves once more.

8 TUESDAY You seem to be at the centre of all activities, both at work and at home. This is the time for pushing ahead with your own needs, asking for a few favours and daring to do what you have only thought about recently. You're attracting financial luck, too, but that's not an excuse to give in to mad gambling. A minor risk is permissible, but anything else would be sheer madness.

9 WEDNESDAY The stars will be providing a stop-go feel about the day; nothing seems to be going according to plan. Naturally, with your meagre allowance of patience it won't take much to make you fly off the handle, and in the heat of the moment you could say something you will regret. The best thing to do is either to spend your day quietly or keep company only with those who have a soothing effect on you.

10 THURSDAY Today Venus will be going into retrograde movement, so from here on in anything connected with your love life, creativity or perhaps matters related to foreign affairs could be extremely complicated. The only thing you can do is to double-check and double-check again. If you do that, you'll have nothing to worry about. Mind you, anyone born under the sign of Libra or Taurus could be downright awkward. Try not to take their words too seriously.

11 FRIDAY Today Mercury will be moving into the sign of Libra, the area of your chart devoted to work and career, where lots of small changes seem to be taking place. Legal matters can be pushed without a second thought. If you have Geminis or Virgos in your circle, they are the people to go to for advice if necessary.

12 SATURDAY The stars seem to have gone potty, because today Saturn is also in retrograde movement. This, of course, is your ruling planet, so for every step you take forward it will be necessary to take half a dozen back. Furthermore, any

♃

friends you have born under the same sign as you are best avoided for the time being; there could be power struggles and bad feelings.

13 SUNDAY Today there could be a tendency for you to blow up minor problems into major disasters and dramas. For heaven's sake calm down, Capricorn, and make a concerted effort to take time to sit and think things through sensibly. In this way you will make life easier, not only for your good self but for those closest to you, who will welcome any effort you make, no matter how small.

14 MONDAY Certainly, because of your willingness to work hard you are likely to be achieving a great deal, but it could be at the expense of your loved ones. They will be accusing you of neglect in the not too distant future. Try to keep a sense of proportion and all should go well.

15 TUESDAY Try as you may to talk common sense into someone close to you, it seems they are not listening, preferring to go their own sweet way. It might be a good idea for you to accept that we all have to 'live and learn'; this certainly seems to be the case right now. Let them get on with their lives while you busy yourself with your own.

16 WEDNESDAY Today Mars will be moving into the airy sign of Libra, the area of your chart devoted to work and career. There may be some tense atmospheres for you to deal with, but at least you have the ability to work hard. The best thing to do is to let other people get on with what is necessary for them, while you do the same for yourself. Whatever you do, don't meddle – otherwise you'll find yourself in hot water.

17 THURSDAY Ulterior motives seem to be at work today, because someone is piling on the flattery and you could easily be fooled by them. As a general rule you can see through others very quickly, just as if they were made of panes of glass, but on this particular day everything seems to be frosted over and your vision is obscured. Be alert to sweet nothings which means just that – nothing.

18 FRIDAY For one reason or another you're not being your usual objective and intelligent self. You are having unrealistically high hopes where a new relationship, or perhaps a pet project, is concerned. It's important that you fight hard to detach yourself so that you can see matters more realistically, then you won't end up disappointed.

19 SATURDAY You may find it more difficult than is usually the case to communicate your wants and needs to other people. It seems that no matter how you try to express yourself, you might as well be talking nonsense. It might be a good idea to keep your demands to a minimum and wait for a better time to sit down and talk things through.

20 SUNDAY While there's no reason why you shouldn't spoil yourself just a little, do try to keep this within the bounds of reason, otherwise you're likely to have your bank manager in floods of tears. If you're planning on visiting him or her, it might be a good idea to take a box of tissues along with you, just in case.

21 MONDAY This is the day of the full Moon, and it occurs in the fiery sign of Aries. This is a time when you will need to put in more effort than usual to achieve your goals. There may be complaints of neglect from those at home, but if you turn on the charm you will probably find them more understanding.

22 TUESDAY Your energy level tends to be a little lower than is usually the case, so you need to keep any strength-sapping activities to a minimum, or even avoid them completely. See what you can do to relax completely. Try to tackle only those things which are of the utmost importance. After all, you can make up for lost time at a later date.

23 WEDNESDAY Certainly, if your work is at all creative, you're going to be reaping the rewards. It's a good time for those in professional partnerships, and many Capricorns will become romantically entangled with people met while going about everyday business. Mind you, there's a certain amount of instability in connection with these relationships. Perhaps you shouldn't take yourself, or other people, too seriously – simply have fun.

24 THURSDAY Today the Sun will be moving into the water sign of Scorpio, the area of your chart devoted to team effort, friends, acquaintances and (to a degree) your ambitions. Mix business with pleasure whenever the chance arises and you'll be doing yourself a lot of good.

25 FRIDAY Today the stars suggest that those closest to you are in a happy-go-lucky frame of mind, so this is not the ideal time for sitting them down and trying to talk common sense or get an important decision out of them. It's best to leave them alone for the time being and perhaps make a fresh approach very soon, when you'll meet with far greater success.

26 SATURDAY Today the stars may be bringing some unexpected opportunities to do yourself a bit of good, which can come completely out of the blue. An older or more experienced person may be involved here; their influence will be beneficial.

27 SUNDAY You have more charm than you know what to do with today. You can push ahead with anything, or anyone, who is dearest to your heart, in the certain knowledge you can succeed. Minor adjustments may be made in your social and romantic plans for the evening. If so, you'll have a touch of magic which will help you to make the most of your time, as well as relationships.

28 MONDAY Today you are much more kind and cherishing than you usually are, but you need to take care that other people don't take advantage of your good mood. This is especially true where the family are concerned. You may have good reason for putting your foot down firmly, although you may be reluctant to do so. This might be the only way you can get them to treat you fairly and justly.

29 TUESDAY The stars suggest that it would be a good idea to avoid making important decisions or major moves, because you really can't see the proverbial wood for the trees. You will have plenty of time later on in the week for pushing ahead. In the mean time, lay down your plans – but don't act on them. Make sure you get in some relaxation this evening.

30 WEDNESDAY You usually know exactly who and what you want out of life, rarely suffering from indecision for longer than a few moments, but now you really seem to be shilly-shallying. Because of this it would be a good idea to let the mood pass before taking any steps which could directly affect your future in an important way. Get out this evening and let off a bit of steam – you need to.

31 THURSDAY It is likely that you will be in the mood for waiting for others to make the next move. However, today is not the right time for forcing the pace in any direction. What you are feeling now is a lack of understanding. What is needed, especially on your part, is a realization that others are struggling with their consciences and their own problems. Perhaps they haven't got sufficient time to give you. That will soon change.

NOVEMBER

Until 21 November the Sun will be coasting along in the water sign of Scorpio, the area of your chart devoted to friends, team effort, acquaintances and, to a degree, the law. All of these areas can be pushed to your heart's content, but don't sit around watching the grass grow.

On the 22nd the Sun will be moving into Sagittarius, the area of your chart devoted to everything that is secret. It will pay you to root around into the background of things in order to find out exactly what's going on. Furthermore, remember that your instincts will not let you down, so force yourself to listen to them if you possibly can – not so easy for you, is it?

Mercury will be in Scorpio up until 18 November. New people will enter your social scene, and any team sports or team efforts are sure to be successful. Push ahead in these areas because you really can't go too far wrong.

♑

From the 19th till the end of the month, Mercury will be residing in Sagittarius. During this period it may be as well to draw in your horns. Stay alert to everything you hear around you – it could come in useful at a later date.

Venus will be in Scorpio all month, throwing a rosy glow on your acquaintanceship circle, your friendships and also casual romance. If there's something special going on at a club you belong to, do pay it a visit because if you happen to be single you could very well find romance. It would be a great pity to miss out, I think you will agree.

Mars has made itself comfortable in Libra, fortunately the area of your chart devoted to work. There's going to be a certain amount of tension and disagreement among work colleagues who may be rivals. The best thing you can do is step back and let them get on with it, because if you stick your nose in, other people will blame you for any friction that's going the rounds. Do the sensible thing and all should be well.

1 FRIDAY The stars are warning you to prepare to give and take more where workmates and colleagues are concerned. Remember, it would also be a good idea to get medical or dental check-ups, particularly if you've forgotten the name of your doctor or dentist.

2 SATURDAY Keep a high profile today, as it is an excellent time for looking for fresh outlets for your talents, especially if you are looking for a permanent job. Those of you in work will be kept rushed off your feet from the moment you arrive to the moment you go home. Because of this you need to spend time this evening with those who are able to bring a smile to your face. It is not the time for romantic decisions.

3 SUNDAY You have an eye for the 'main chance' and are likely to be getting in touch with people who, you believe, can help you push ahead with your ambitions. A mixture of business and pleasure seems likely; on the other hand, you need to be wary of neglecting your loved ones, or you'll be making yourself unpopular. Make sure you include them in your plans.

4 MONDAY Today is the day of the new Moon, and it occurs in the watery sign of Scorpio. This could mean you'll be meeting new contacts and friends, as well as acquaintances, either at work or perhaps in your personal life. Either way, these people will have a beneficial and positive effect on you, so don't hesitate to make friends.

5 TUESDAY The stars are certainly gingering you up and you're being a busy little bee, but it's important that you don't have too many fingers in too many pies – a common fault. Sort out your priorities and distinguish that which is important from that which is pure trivia. Being active is fine, but not if you're simply running around in circles; you'll just end up angry and frustrated.

6 WEDNESDAY The stars are filling you with solar power, energy and confidence, and also increasing your sense of humour. If you've anything important to do today, don't hesitate to act because you simply can't go wrong. This evening, local activities are likely to appeal, and brief encounters are more than just a possibility. It's likely you'll be on the go from morning till night, and thoroughly enjoying yourself too.

♑

7 THURSDAY You've been reasonably sensible with money for quite some time now, considering you can be a little scatty from time to time. However, this is one day when you can spoil yourself a little, but do make certain that you don't go completely over the top as is frequently the case due to your expensive tastes.

8 FRIDAY Your relationships, particularly partnerships, are well starred. This is a great time for co-operating with other people wherever possible. You may begin the day feeling a little lazy and unenthusiastic, but somebody else's enthusiasm rubs off on you in a big way. Be ready to go for what you want out of life, because you can almost certainly get it in the near future.

9 SATURDAY You've enough energy to light up Buckingham Palace and the White House combined. Others will naturally gravitate towards you, and because of this it's a great time for asking for favours and pushing your luck where romance is concerned, particularly if you have been holding an enormous torch for somebody for a long time. Get out and let yourself go.

10 SUNDAY Any immediate worries that you have must be attended to, because your imagination and your intuition are spot on and it is a great day for making one or two serious decisions, particularly if they are connected with your family, love life or property. Having done so, you'll be feeling quite pleased with yourself and will be ready to give yourself over to fun and games.

b

11 MONDAY There are likely to be a lot of changes in the lives of those closest to you, and plenty of news coming from them which will re-kindle an old ambition and set you off chasing your dreams and wishes over the next couple of days. Believe in yourself, Capricorn, because you can move mountains.

12 TUESDAY A phone call, or perhaps a letter, from abroad seems to be one of the highlights of the day. This is a great time for considering ways of improving yourself, either physically (by trying a new look) or mentally (by signing up for a fresh course of learning). A social invitation this evening is likely to lead to romance, so you should accept immediately. You could be in for a memorable time.

13 WEDNESDAY The planets will bring you changes of mind throughout the day; this could lead in turn to a change of direction. Sit down and work out what is practical, sensible and lucrative, and separate it from what is wishful thinking or that which is impractical. A few moments alone will help you to distinguish one from the other.

14 THURSDAY What you need to do is to work out what needs to be done today, and then leap into action. This evening, where possible try to get out and enjoy yourself in the company of friends, because this is one way you might be able to find romance, as well as maximum enjoyment for minimum financial outlay.

15 FRIDAY The stars are encouraging you to be more creative, but also perhaps a little too idealistic. Certainly the former can be used in order to impress those people who count, but the latter might result in you expecting too much of yourself and other people too.

16 SATURDAY During this day it's definitely going to be a case of whom you know and not what you know which will aid your progress. It's a particularly lucky time if you work as a member of a team, because some kind of breakthrough is a possibility. Your friendship circle is likely to be growing, and your popularity won't be in question. You're going to be rushed off your feet.

17 SUNDAY Recent difficulties or misunderstandings with relatives can be swept to one side at this time. All you need to do is pocket your pride and open your mind as well as your heart. Luckily, you shouldn't find it difficult to do either and your day should be a good one. If you're entertaining friends at home this evening, this will not only prove to be fun, but rewarding in some way.

18 MONDAY There's no point in you being too independent today, neither is there any point in just drifting around without any chosen direction. What you should be doing is considering the wants and needs of other people. Luckily you'll find this relatively easy to do. If you're visiting any sort of club this evening, you should enjoy yourself; you may even find romance.

19 TUESDAY Cash matters only improve if you can persuade yourself to push ahead with your great money making ideas. Stop being so negative and fearing the worst, be your usual self and let other people know what you are thinking, they are likely to be impressed. Nobody is going to think you are being pushy when they see how spot on your judgement is today.

20 WEDNESDAY Others around you, no matter where you go, seem to be very energetic. Because of this you may have to run just to keep pace with them. Mind you, you'll find all this activity extremely stimulating, because you like to keep on the move. This is also a time which will be extremely important for romance, so many of you should be prepared to be swept off your feet.

21 THURSDAY If you want to make any changes to your life you've a perfect day for doing just that. It's a good time, too, if you've money to spare, because somebody will be handing on a snippet of information which could turn into a solid investment – and we're not talking about backing some three-legged horse. If you have made a social arrangement some time ago, it might be a good idea to do a little double-checking, because changes may have occurred in the lives of the people you were planning to spend time with, and this may necessitate a re-think.

22 FRIDAY Today the Sun will be moving into the fiery sign of Sagittarius, the area of your chart devoted to what's going on behind the scenes. Furthermore, your instincts are going to be unbeatable at this time. The only problem is, are we going to be able to persuade you to use them? I certainly hope so, otherwise you'll be kicking yourself for the next couple of weeks or so, which would be a shame.

23 SATURDAY Luckily your judgement is spot on; those around you are going to be impressed. If you're waiting for news from abroad, perhaps in the form of a phone call, you shouldn't be disappointed. There's a novel feel about this evening and you're likely to be spending your time in the company of people you don't know that well.

24 SUNDAY Your energy levels are ridiculously high, so you need to channel them constructively or you could become bad-tempered or achieve precious little. What's more, this is a great time for chasing potential lovers because you'll find that they will allow themselves to be caught. Naturally, if you're in a relationship this could be a dangerous time, so don't give in to temptation. You'll regret it if you do.

25 MONDAY Take advantage of the fact that your concentration levels have increased. You couldn't have a more perfect time for laying down plans for the future, or making changes in your life which you deem necessary. You might be out and about socializing but, if so, you'll be taking your pleasures far more seriously than is usually the case. Others will wonder what has come over you.

26 TUESDAY You'll be taking your emotions more seriously than is usual. Some of you may have become rather bored with simply leaping around with a new face every other day, because you suddenly realize this is not the way to get to know anybody in real depth. If you're fancy-free, you may very well be drawn to those who are more experienced or older than yourself, simply because you will feel you can learn a great deal from them, and can't resist the opportunity to acquire knowledge.

27 WEDNESDAY Where possible you'll stick to the routine today, because you want to leave plenty of energy and enthusiasm for your evening activities. Among these, romance is likely to be at the top of your list of priorities. It won't be hard to find. In fact, you could discover several admirers, but you mustn't give in to the temptation to form multiple relationships. This will only make your life unnecessarily complicated, and though you may enjoy it at first, it could prove to be a real pain in the neck.

28 THURSDAY Other people at work, at home and in your love life are more confident, giving and helpful. So, Capricorn, if you need any sort of favour this is the time to pluck up your courage and ask for it, because it will most certainly be granted. The evening is a fantastic time for romance.

29 FRIDAY It might seem time to make some world-shattering decisions, but these should be left for the time being. In the mean while, put the finishing touches to work, projects or relationships because, let's face it, there is a tendency for you on occasion to leave things undone. See what you can do.

30 SATURDAY The stars are likely to bring new contacts into your life, and they will fast become close friends. And, because of the influence of somebody new, you could develop a new ambition and will be excitedly making plans with them. This is a great time for fresh thoughts.

DECEMBER

Until 21 December the Sun this month will be drifting along in the fiery sign of Sagittarius, the area of your chart which

℞

represents everything that is hidden from view. I'm not saying you should go out looking for trouble, but if you suspect that somebody is talking a load of old rubbish and trying to involve you in any kind of scheme, you should do a lot of investigating. Otherwise you may end up wishing you'd never got in involved in the first place. In your personal life, listen to your instincts, something you very rarely do but something which will pay off well this month. You'll know exactly when other people are being sincere and when they are just giving you a whole lot of 'bull'.

On 22 December the Sun will be moving into your own sign. This is your time of year, when you have utmost confidence. You must be quick to make the most of this. You're looking good, feeling good and have faith in everything you say or do, and because of this other people will believe you too – not that you would ever give out false information, that's not your style. You usually cogitate everything and may only come down on one side or the other when you know what you're talking about. This is certainly the case right now.

Mercury will be in the fiery sign of Sagittarius until 8 December, and your imagination is running riot. Let yourself be led by your intuition and you won't go far wrong. Mercury will then be in your sign from the 9th, enlivening your whole personality and making it a good time for dealing with youngsters, legal matters and any kind of travel. If you have a Virgo or a Gemini in your life, they're going to be a positive boon, especially when you're looking for advice. Don't hesitate to go to them; you'll regret it if you don't.

Venus will be in Scorpio this month, throwing a rosy glow over team effort, friendship, acquaintances, your bank and all kinds of legal matters. Any or all of these can be tackled with alacrity because you are full of confidence and know what you're talking about. Nobody's going to suggest otherwise.

Mars will also be in Scorpio from the 2nd. This is a very sexy combination, so from time to time you may wonder what on earth has come over you, as indeed will other people, because the Goat is usually very serene, quiet and unassuming – not now, you'll be making your mark whenever you possibly can, and why not? It'll shake other people up and they'll stop taking you for granted, which, quite frankly, can be no bad thing, as I'm sure you'll agree.

The pattern made by the stars suggests that the majority of the influences in life are going to be affecting your home, your family and perhaps your offspring, if you have any. Romance will be relatively well starred, but not exactly 'out of this world', so do keep one trotter on the ground. If you don't, you'll get hurt, and nobody aches as much as a Capricorn when it's treated in such a cavalier fashion. You can avoid this with just a little bit of caution.

1 SUNDAY Today it's up to you to make sure that other people are listening to your creative ideas. Take your inspirations and one-off notions and do the done thing. You were born under the sign of tenacity; now is the time to let your boss and everybody else know about it by stepping into the limelight. There's no harm in occasionally letting other people realize just how clever you are, as long as you don't overdo it. By communicating and hustling you're living up to your reputation as an ambitious person, so make sure that other people realize that it is your ideas they really want.

2 MONDAY Concentration could be elusive; the best way to side-step trouble is not to turn your attention to anything which requires a good deal of time or effort because, if you do, you'll be making mistakes which you could live to regret in a big way. You may find it difficult to understand yourself at the moment; it's best not to try in the first place. Simply roll with the punches, Capricorn, and everything should be fine.

3 TUESDAY Today, Capricorn, is the day for trying to make a breakthrough in the direction of your wants and desires for the future, otherwise you could miss out on an opportunity which will be a long time coming your way again. Think positively, all you need is that extra touch of confidence in order to succeed. Remember, you're as good as anybody, perhaps even better. If you bear this thought in mind, you can't possibly fail.

4 WEDNESDAY Rest assured that somewhere in the back of your mind you have the answer to most of your problems. Your only difficulty is locating them, so take time to think things through. It's possible that you're allowing worry to throw you off-course. This simply won't do if you are to succeed.

5 THURSDAY There are so many good aspects today, it's difficult to know where to start. You're in top form, so make sure you pay attention to yourself and your talents. Refuse to be intimidated by anybody at all, no matter how much you may care for them. Of course, it goes without saying that you must be tactful when declining offers. Nevertheless, stay rock solid throughout the day. This is a good time for beginning anything new.

6 FRIDAY The reason you're so popular is because you're so friendly and, for the most part, outgoing. You're generally quite happy to talk to anybody. You can succeed in at least one important area by yourself right now, though certainly you may be tested along the road, either by emotional problems of your own or by other people. Overcome this and you'll be on the way to finding success.

7 SATURDAY In order to succeed you need a sharp mind as well as ambition, so it's pretty lucky that, astrologically speaking, you have both, particularly at this time. You're now going through a period when you must prepare for success in the future and adjust yourself to any changes which occur. Be prepared for anything, Capricorn, you can succeed.

8 SUNDAY Other people will be making adjustments to plans and arrangements and, providing they don't overstep the mark, you will be quite happy to trot along at their behest. People you meet today will have an overwhelming effect on you, but it is likely to be only temporary – but then, it takes a great deal to affect you at a deep level.

9 MONDAY Today Mercury will be entering Capricorn and that, of course, is your own sign. You're going to be much more flexible and adaptable during the days ahead. Furthermore, it's a good time for tackling anything connected with legal matters or travel, so don't hesitate to do so. If you have a fellow Capricorn in your circle, this is the person to go to if you need any kind of advice, because they know exactly 'where you're coming from'.

10 TUESDAY Watch your step where romance is concerned, because other people may not be strictly up-front with you. If you meet anyone new, be sure to check on their marital status. Although you haven't any problem with a one-night stand with someone who is committed elsewhere, you certainly don't want to become embroiled in an 'eternal triangle', because that makes life too complicated, which, in turn, brings difficulties you can well do without.

11 WEDNESDAY Today nothing will be straightforward in your love life or where socializing is concerned, so don't take anything for granted. The more double-checking you do today, the better. This advice also applies to those of you involved in creative work, because mistakes could be made in this direction too. This is clearly not a day for taking anything, or anyone, at face value.

12 THURSDAY You're likely to be entering the gates of opportunity, and have a choice either to stroll right in or simply knock in the hope that somebody will open them for you. Do take a calculated risk; you have nothing to lose and everything to gain and, with your tremendous enthusiasm, optimism and great ideas, you have the perfect personality to make things happen. Support from a friend or a partner will also be useful, so don't hesitate to pick their brains if this will help you in any way.

13 FRIDAY Today the stars suggest you avoid taking anything connected to family or property for granted. In these areas of life, minor new changes seem to be taking place. Be your usual adaptable self and you'll cope. Home entertaining will be a good idea this evening.

14 SATURDAY You could fall foul of a bout a self-deception today; it might be a good idea to shelve important decisions and intricate work until you are able to put at least one little

β

toe on terra firma. Don't go out of your way to make life more complicated than it already is, there's a Capricorn tendency in you to do so simply out of a strong sense of duty, or sometimes mischief.

15 SUNDAY Your concentration could break down at any moment today; the best thing to do is to shelve anything which is detailed or needs more than half an hour of your time. Far better to hop from one thing to another, as it's unlikely you'll believe everything you are told by people who are unfamiliar to you. Better to stick with your old friends instead.

16 MONDAY There may be a degree of muddle in routine work. Workmates could be cranky or even downright disagreeable, so get on with your own business and allow them to do the same. If you're feeling at all tired this evening, try to get an early night. Naturally this goes against the grain, but even you need a period of recuperation, and this could be it.

17 TUESDAY Today you tend to be attracted to situations and people who are a little 'different'. You should stay on the conventional side of life right now, however. You're in just the sort of mood to deal with everyday matters exceptionally well, because you have your feet on the ground and people are keen to work with you. Certainly your personality is bubbling beneath the surface, but make sure that it doesn't burst forth.

18 WEDNESDAY Turn your attention to the areas of your life that don't depend too much on emotion, or you'll end up in a confused state. By keeping your feet firmly on the ground where business or work is concerned, you are able to deal with people and situations in a manner that produces confidence and commitment in you. If you wander off into the realms of 'what might have been', you'll miss out on a lot of opportunities which are right under your nose.

19 THURSDAY The stars are filling you with confidence and positive thinking, and your sense of humour will certainly help to aid your progress. Force yourself into being a little more daring and don't think twice about presenting your ideas or suggestions to others. The evening is a time for keeping a high profile, because if you do you'll be attracting in a big way, and that's exactly what you want.

20 FRIDAY Someone you haven't seen for a while is likely to be getting in touch with interesting news or gossip. If you have been lonely recently, you'll find this a great time for getting closer to others, relaxing and generally boosting your flagging morale. This won't be hard to do, providing you are selective.

21 SATURDAY Complications or disagreements you may have had with friends, acquaintances or contacts will become a thing of the past over the next few days or so. Luckily, you don't suffer from foolish pride and so, if you believe that you have been in the wrong, you're very quick to say so and will be gaining a great deal in the way of admiration.

22 SUNDAY Today the Sun will be moving into your own sign, so you're beginning a few weeks when you're looking good, feeling good and will be drawing attention to your talents. Do not be a modest Goat, go out there and be a little

ß

bit more flamboyant. Make others sit up and listen, and it'll be a long time before they take you for granted again, I can assure you.

23 MONDAY The best thing to do now is to attend to routine work and set aside anything which requires a great deal of effort or imagination, because you are short on these commodities at the moment. Ideally you should relax this evening, but naturally, as a Capricorn, you will force yourself out and about. You'll tire quickly, though, and will return home sooner than you expected.

24 TUESDAY Today is, of course, Christmas Eve. Now, if you are a parent you'll be running around trying to do the best you can for your offspring. However, if you run yourself into the ground the family will not be best pleased when Christmas Day arrives and all you want to do is sleep. Try to keep a sense of proportion and all should be well.

25 WEDNESDAY Happy Christmas! This is the day you've worked and slaved for over recent months. Mind you, with any luck you're likely to be more satisfied with the reaction you get from loved ones, family and friends than you have over recent years, so all of that effort will be stimulating you to give of your best and help other people enjoy themselves – just the right attitude for Christmas, of course.

26 THURSDAY This, of course, is the day when most of us can relax just a touch. Hopefully you didn't eat too much – as a Goat, of course, you frequently do. If you're feeling a little bit 'fragile', be kind to yourself today because, let's face it, New Year's Eve is only just around the corner.

ђ

27 FRIDAY Today thoughts will occasionally turn to work, but that's the wrong attitude to have at this time and it'll only make your family irritated. Therefore, don't even mention that four-letter word; instead, try to find out what you can do to make them happy, or what is bothering them. After all, we've always got plenty of time on our hands on this day, so why don't you use it constructively?

28 SATURDAY Once more, work is still on your mind and workmates may even dare to ring you up. If so, you'd better not let your partner or family know, otherwise they will go through the ceiling – and who could blame them? Give the loved ones in your life lots of attention and lots of cuddles, and you will have a happy time.

29 SUNDAY The phone goes mad today and it looks as if your friends are fed up with sitting at home during the cold weather, so it's quite likely that they might be angling for an invitation to see you. If you sense this, then invite them round. You don't have to put on a banquet, a bit of cold turkey – if you've still got some – or perhaps something a little fresher, plus a little drop of wine will do fine.

30 MONDAY The stars today suggest that you may be thinking about work and making plans for the future. Your recent activities are beginning to catch up with you and you need time to catch your breath. Don't allow other people to make you feel guilty if you decide to laze around thinking, but not acting. No doubt after a couple of hours of inactivity you'll be itching to get started again, and although you had promised yourself an early night, it's doubtful that you'll stick to this because the mood for fun suddenly descends.

31 TUESDAY You could be finding adventurous ways to celebrate the new year; you'll even be prepared to travel quite a distance in order to have fun, or perhaps even find romance, and why shouldn't you? Those of you who must stay at home for one reason or another are sure to be receiving a long-distance telephone call that will make your evening; it's always nice to know that loved ones haven't forgotten us. If you're acting as host or hostess this evening, make sure that your partner lends a hand. When all's said and done, you're only one person. Even though you can achieve more than five others, it still may not be enough to get everything done. Pace yourself, Capricorn, and have a Happy New Year!